CLASSIC
DESIGN STYLES

Henrietta Spencer-Churchill

CLASSIC DESIGN STYLES

PERIOD LIVING FOR TODAY'S INTERIORS

HENRIETTA SPENCER-CHURCHILL

CICO BOOKS

London

First published in Great Britain by
Cico Books
32 Great Sutton Street
London EC1V 0NB
Copyright © Cico Books 2001

Text copyright © Henrietta Spencer-Churchill 2001

10 9 8 7 6 5 4 3 2 1

A CIP catalogue record for this book is available from the British Library

ISBN 1 903116 25 2

Managing Editor: Georgina Harris

Styling: Rose Hammick

Editor: Ian Kearey

Design: Christine Wood

Printed and bound in Singapore by Kyodo

CONTENTS

INTRODUCTION

Restoring a period house, or embarking on building a new one in a period style, can be a daunting process; especially

if, like myself, you are passionate about architectural detail from the greatest periods of British and North American

culture and determined to leave no stone unturned in your quest to get it right.

It is our duty as keepers of centuries-old national traditions to respect and preserve our heritage, which is why cer-

tain period buildings are protected, and fortunately have restrictions placed on what can and cannot be done to them.

For these reasons, in order to understand and restore your home, you may well need to carry out your own research

and discover how it has evolved over the years. This can be a long process and may require assistance from profes-

sionals or local archives. Nonetheless, for the house to work as a whole it is essential to get the 'bones' , or

architectural details, right first; and during your search you may also discover aspects of the house that were

not apparent before.

It is only natural that houses evolve and change over the centuries, incorporating many different periods and styles,

and consequently a strictly purist approach is wrong and cannot be made to work; it is therefore perfectly acceptable

to add your own improvement and alterations – so long as they are sympathetic to the core of the structure.

Unfortunately, it is becoming increasingly difficult – and expensive – to acquire period details to replicate or replace those that would have been found in previous generations or are suitable for the period of the house.

Given these restrictions, I see nothing wrong in recreating details to achieve what you want: today, we are fortunate to have many skilled craftsmen and companies who can perfectly replicate anything from eighteenth-century plaster mouldings to seventeenth-century wood panelling, and in the future these details will one day be recognized and preserved by our great-great-grandchildren.

At the end of the day you want your house to be a home, to reflect your own style, and one in which you feel comfortable. The purpose of this book is to give you ideas when recreating a period room or renovating a whole house; it is not meant to dictate the correctness of a certain style, but to inspire.

You will see how styles have developed over the centuries and how they can be interpreted for today's living, whether town or country, cottage or manor house, English or American. With versatility, you can pick and choose your ideas – a wall treatment or colour from one room, a window treatment from another – to create your own harmonious look, and hopefully have fun in the process!

Henrietta Spencer-Churchill

CLASSIC DESIGN STYLES

The houses and decorations in this section are drawn from over eight

centuries, from the open great halls and spaces of the Medieval period

to the delicate craftsmanship of the late-nineteenth-century

Arts and Crafts movement. Each of these eras has its adherents and

enthusiasts, and each can be studied and visited as a separate

architectural and decorative style. However, for most of us who live in

a period house or building, it is the mixing and matching that excite

us, blending the original style and features with the best of

modern-day comfort and convenience.

Above: Italian Renaissance wall motif

Left: The combination of dark panelled walls, subtle, muted lighting, well-chosen furniture and furnishings, and an imposing fireplace make a Victorian drawing room a welcoming setting.

MEDIEVAL STYLE

Early-Medieval architecture was influenced by ecclesiastical buildings, with large two- or three-storey great halls proving the hub around which the everyday life of the house revolved. Heat was provided by a central fire placed in the middle of the hall, with the smoke being allowed to escape through louvres in the roof – during the twelfth and thirteenth centuries windows were small and little more than narrow slits. Because of this, floors needed to be durable, and were made of hard plaster or compressed earth covered with rushes. The discomfort of draughty, smoke-filled rooms led to the introduction of wall fireplaces in the fifteenth century; floors could thus become more of a feature, and were often made of painted clay tiles or wooden boards.

The need for effective insulation led to the introduction of wooden wainscoting in the later part of the thirteenth century. At first this was simple tongue-and-groove boards or square panels, often painted; this style lasted until the introduction of elaborate woodcarving, such as linenfold panelling, toward the end of the fifteenth century. At the same time, the desire for greater privacy and comfort led to the development of additional living quarters within the house, where the family could sleep, work and wash; the servants were contained in service areas where food was prepared and provisions were stored.

Carved detail, Medieval ceiling

Left: Medieval styles evoke a look of sparseness and open, uncluttered space, with high-vaulted or beamed ceilings. The style is not grand, but it can be awe-inspiring. Create warmth with the use of rich, earthy tones of limewashed, plastered or colourwashed walls, with bare timbering or wainscoting at the base of the wall.

Right: Throughout the Medieval period it was typical to leave beams and roof timbers exposed, with perhaps some decorative paintwork. You can recreate the colour and decoration once supplied solely by wall hangings by using paintings that have the warm, rustic tones so reminiscent of the period, which blend in with dried flowers and plants strung along the beams.

Right: Medieval walls were whitewashed or rendered with plaster of Paris painted to simulate stonework, and were adorned with hand-painted flowers or heraldic designs. Background tones were largely of earth and white. Dress earthenware tiles or wide oak plank floors with rugs in coir matting or woven rushes.

Furniture was sparse, so colour and decoration were provided by large wall hangings, made from wood and linen and painted with shields and coats of arms. Elaborate tapestries and embroidered wool and silk wall hangings were used later, often imported from France and the Low Countries. Hangings were used to keep out draughts, to dress beds, to provide privacy and warmth, and to give significance and importance to areas such as the dais at one side of the hall, or as a canopy over the landlord's chair.

As most noblemen and wealthier landowners were always on the move, possessions were sparse, precious and needed to be transportable. After the bed, trestle tables with benches and stools were the most common items of furniture, along with chests and coffers, which were used for storage at home and as trunks on the move.

Gothic Hall chair

Carved oak dining chair

RENAISSANCE STYLE

Italian Renaissance wall motif

The creation of smaller rooms and a desire for greater privacy and comfort continued into the sixteenth century, and styles of architecture followed a greater influence from Europe, in particular the Italian Renaissance. Tudor houses were still built around the great hall, but the parlour took over as the main room for dining and everyday use.

Rooms, although not so large, had bigger windows, and glass was now affordable and accessible to the less wealthy. Gothic tracery and stone arches were replaced by stone mullions with rectangular panes; stained glass remained popular in grander houses. The fireplace was the main focal point in the room, and during the Tudor period its shape frequently supported the traditional Gothic arch, but with additional elaborate carvings of European Renaissance influence. The Elizabethans favoured more classical designs, with carved columns and caryatids made from wood, stone or marble.

On walls the linenfold pattern became more and more elaborate, incorporating details such as lace edging. Panelling extended to a greater height on the wall, in many cases incorporating a carved or plaster-moulded frieze, often painted. Grander houses used hardwoods such as oak, while smaller houses used painted pine. Wallpaper appeared in the early sixteenth century as small panels that were often pasted onto linen before being applied to the walls. Floors were made from local stone, with slate or marble on display in grander houses.

Left: Panelled rooms, usually of oak, are typical of Renaissance style. Panelled wood can be made lighter by bleaching to remove a build-up of dark wax or varnish. Oak furniture with turned legs and carved panels is appropriate, if expensive in its original form. Accurate reproductions are available and affordable.

Carved Italian chair

Brick was also used, but was not so durable. Oak and elm boards were found predominantly on the upper floors, which were left bare. Loose rushes had been replaced with rush matting, and 'Turkey work' carpets were found in some grander houses.

The desire for comfort and practical living led to the introduction of static or custom built-in furniture. Recesses or niches were turned into cupboards with the addition of a simple frame and doors, and benches were often placed in window recesses or adjacent to fireplaces. Furniture was mostly made from oak or elm, with the occasional piece of walnut. Accessories became more abundant too, with cushions on chairs and benches, and cloths on tables giving a more luxurious feel. Rooms were lit with candlelight.

Plaster ceiling motif

Left: With great halls no longer paramount, two-storey rooms gave way to single-height rooms with ceilings of lath and plaster. Leave these plain in less important rooms, or decorate them with elaborate friezes supporting motifs of floral and animal forms, as well as Gothic heraldic shields.

Right: Later Elizabethan and Jacobean ceilings followed the form of elaborate carved wooden ceilings of the Tudor period – use plasterwork and intricate mouldings to create strapwork ceilings. Keep curtains simple and hanging on metal or wood poles.

BAROQUE STYLE

The Baroque period in England witnessed a huge change in the way houses were built

and architecture and design were executed. During the course of the seventeenth century,

'decorum' (a sense of appropriateness) was reinstated in the way in which houses were

built. This process started with the English architect Inigo Jones, whose understanding

of the Classical disciplines of order and sense of proportion influenced craftsmen.

Carved Baroque chairback

The trend for combining Classical architecture with flamboyant decoration started in

Italy and spread throughout Europe, with Italian craftsmen creating elaborate interiors

that combined sinuous curves with Classical lines and ornate frescoes and stucco.

Houses were built with a new lavishness, and the internal layout was changed to adopt a

more courtly, social style. The main entertaining rooms were placed on the *piano nobile*,

effectively a raised ground floor, while service rooms were confined to the basement,

with additional bedrooms and servants' quarters in the attic.

The desire for symmetry on the façade of a house also dictated its internal layout.

The great hall became a vestibule, with the main staircase leading to the main rooms.

Some grander houses had an external staircase leading directly to the *piano nobile*, where

large rooms were ornately decorated with *trompe-l'oeil* paintings and gilded stucco. The

emphasis was on great internal detail. By the late seventeenth century most ceilings were

plastered, and naturalistic motifs replaced the geometric designs favoured by the

Left: The contrast between the dark wooden furniture and panelling and the
pale walls and columns is a characteristically Baroque effect.

Ornate Baroque court chair

Baroque moulded wall frieze

Jacobeans. Wall panelling was still popular, but became less constricted. Inigo Jones had introduced floor-to-ceiling pilasters, but now there were panels with a continuous dado rail around the room, and decorative cornices and mouldings.

Panelling was still painted – in grand houses it was gilded, and in modest rooms grained like wood, or marbled. The rooms on the ground floor tended to be stone, with oak or deal floorboards preferred for upstairs rooms. Parquet flooring was introduced, but carpets remained scarce. Interior furnishings were greatly influenced by France, in particular the use of a single fabric for walls, bed hangings and cushions. Curtains, hung on rods, were more commonplace, and the pull-up curtain, referred to as 'festoon', was used in grand rooms. The bed was still the most important piece of furniture and was dressed with ornate fabrics, such as silk damasks, brocatelles and embroidered crewelwork. Many other pieces of furniture were produced, and walnut replaced oak as the most favoured wood, sometimes inlaid with marquetry.

Dining-room um

Left: Baroque rooms could incorporate a huge variety of different styles in wooden panelling, with further variations in stone and marble. Rounded and squared columns and pilasters could also appear side by side.

Right: The magnificence of this stone and marble fireplace is equalled by the sumptuous frieze-to-floor wall hangings, with an abundance of pure gold embroidery. Allegorical statues were a popular feature.

QUEEN ANNE STYLE

By the beginning of the eighteenth century, the excesses of the Baroque period began to

go out of fashion and were replaced by the simple, more elegant lines of the early

Palladian style. Queen Anne's reign lasted for only twelve years and the period did not

witness any great architectural changes, but it was characterized by a desire for simple,

elegant taste and comfortable surroundings, which lasted well into the eighteenth

century and led the way for the Georgian and Empire styles.

Queen Anne style is refined and delicate and evokes harmony, comfort and elegance.

Works of art and furniture produced during this time possessed infinite detail, with fine

veneering replacing the heavier marquetry of the previous period. Ornate, turned legs on

tables and chairs were replaced by more elegant cabriole legs, often with bell or claw

feet. Many new pieces of furniture that were designed and made in the early 1700s are

still in use or reproduced today. It was the age of walnut, and fine examples of chests of

drawers, tallboys, games tables and side tables were made. The style spread to America

in the 1750s, while the delicacy and detail were revived in Britain in the late-Victorian era.

Symmetry and balance were all-important in the placement of furniture within a

room. Panelled rooms were either painted in subtle shades of one colour to emphasize

Early-18th-century English cabinet

Queen Anne chair design

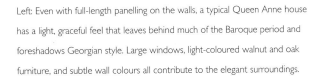

Left: Even with full-length panelling on the walls, a typical Queen Anne house
has a light, graceful feel that leaves behind much of the Baroque period and
foreshadows Georgian style. Large windows, light-coloured walnut and oak
furniture, and subtle wall colours all contribute to the elegant surroundings.

the panels or, if pine and previously painted, were stripped back and waxed or limed.

Where hardwood panelling, usually made from mahogany or walnut, was used, it was

not polished too dark, as rich, heavy colours were deemed to be more suitable as a

backdrop for walnut furniture. Where cheaper woods were used for panelling, they

were often marbled or grained.

Wall hangings were usually silk, damask, velvet or tapestry, although grand houses

display sets of painted leather panels. The earliest hand-blocked wallpapers were being

produced in small quantities; these were often hand-coloured. In addition, pulverized

cloth was used to make flock wallpaper.

New and inexpensive methods of production, such as moulds that were used to

mass-manufacture plaster decorations, were introduced at the beginning of the

eighteenth century, so even less grand houses could now feature a certain amount of

plasterwork. Scagliola, a composite plaster imitation of marble and other stones, was

popular for floors and columns.

Although curtains were still not very common at this time, bare windows could

feel bleak, so simple fabrics were hung on a pole, or stiff, elegant pelmets were

used, often in conjunction with wooden window shutters. Fabrics were plain

linens, damasks and velvets – printed fabrics were not yet available – and the

same fabrics were also employed for upholstery, while bare wooden floorboards

were covered by rugs.

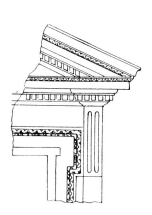

Classical column and roof detail

Plaster cornicing detail

Right: The Queen Anne
period saw a refinement of the
elaborate plasterwork
mouldings that epitomized
the Baroque era. Paint most
mouldings white, but pick
them out in gold in grander
rooms or houses.

EARLY GEORGIAN STYLE

The Early Georgian period is characterized by the emphasis that was placed on Classical architectural detail. The leading proponents of the Palladian style were the English gentlemen William Kent and Lord Burlington, and they left nothing to chance. Entire rooms were designed, from the walls and ceilings to every piece of furniture. Scale, proportion and balance were key factors in design, and room sizes were calculated in terms of cubes.

The main staircase became much more of a feature in the hall than in Baroque days, and was typically wooden with carved balusters. Grander houses might have a stone cantilevered staircase with a wrought-iron balustrade.

Panelled rooms still prevailed, but the mouldings tended to be of plaster with elegant cornices and friezes. Certain styles and motifs were popular, such as egg and dart, acanthus leaf,

Left: Mirrors were used in Georgian drawing rooms as decoration and to reflect and double the candle power.

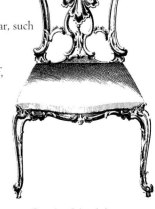

Georgian dining chair

27

dentil and Greek key, and these motifs were repeated on door and window architraves, shutters and fireplaces, as well as on furniture.

In more modest houses panelling was predominantly softwood painted in soft, muted colours, such as duck-egg blue, olive green, buff and brown. Bolection moulding gave way to raised-and-fielded panels, stimulating a more restrained use of paint techniques. At the beginning of the period walls were still covered in panelling, but later this was restricted to dado height only, with fabric, paint or paper covering the rest of the wall.

As Englishmen began to travel abroad more extensively, possessions were acquired and rooms to house them in gained importance: galleries for paintings, halls and corridors with specially designed niches for sculpture and statuary, and libraries for books, increased. New furniture for these spaces and rooms was produced, stimulating new heights in craftsmanship. Upholstered pieces, such as the fauteuil, were introduced from France.

Toward the middle of the eighteenth century the asymmetrical Rococo style began to be seen in England. Its flowing, curved lines, with scrolls, ribbons and shell motifs, were initially reserved for stucco work on ceilings and walls.

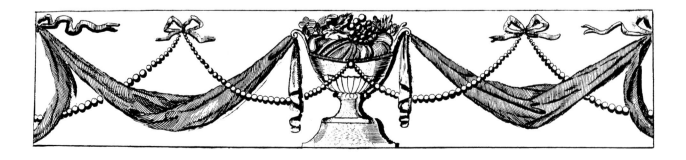

COLONIAL STYLE

Colonial style covers the period in North America from the 1650s to the 1770s. Before

this time, the first settlers were forced to create homes as quickly as possible, so designs

were rudimentary and materials were limited.

The basic layouts and principles of Colonial houses differed very little from those in

England, the main differences being the use of materials and the fact that ideas took

longer to spread across the Atlantic – and therefore prevailed longer. Later Colonial

designs were influenced by pattern books imported from England. European influences

might govern the style, but American builders added their own interpretations. Wood

was more readily available than brick or stone, especially on the East Coast, where houses

were clad with sawn weatherboards or clapboards and roofs were made of shingles.

Brick was used only for chimneys and decoration, and stone was used for grand houses.

In the South, houses had steeply pitched gables with dormer windows and stone or

brick chimneys at each end. Most were one room deep and one storey high, with a large,

open attic space. New England houses resembled those from Renaissance England, with

small windows, low ceilings, a large central fireplace and exposed beams.

Left: An unusual but effective
way to decorate plain,
unadorned plaster walls is to
paint a mural that creates a
strong atmosphere.

Engraved wine glass

Palladian-style houses, with symmetrical façades, sash windows with shutters, and central halls, were seen in America from the mid-eighteenth century, and were usually built by wealthy plantation owners in the south. The designs were based on pattern books by James Gibbs and William Salmon, and gradually brick replaced wood for the principal elevations. A typical American Georgian feature was the steeply pitched roof with dormer windows, influenced by Dutch settlers, which lasted into the next century.

Wood was used for most interior details, from panelling and fireplaces to staircases and floors. Early, modest houses might only have the fireplace wall panelled, the others being plastered; both were painted in earthy tones, as the use of wallpapers and fabrics had not come into vogue. Cornices and skirtings were introduced when plaster ceilings became common in the early eighteenth century. Plain, unstained floors of pine were used throughout, while stone floors were rare and limited to porches or halls. Before carpets became commonplace, painted floorcloths were more typically used to cover the boards than rush matting.

Built-in furniture was designed to be both functional and aesthetic, with an upper section for display, often featuring a decorative pediment and columns, and a plainer, more practical storage area below. Cabinetmaking developed regionally: designs inspired by European pattern books were often simplified, and a more individual, American style came into being, using locally available walnut, chestnut and cherry. Much Colonial furniture was painted decoratively, the designs inspired by folk art from Dutch and Scandinavian settlers.

Early Colonial tallboy

Right: Native American woods were used for the Colonial chairs, table and mirror, as well as for the painted panelling and decorative built-in storage space, with its fluted columns and scallop top.

EMPIRE STYLE

Although 'Empire style' covers the era up to the Victorian period, it can be divided

into two related styles: late Georgian and Regency. The Neo-Classical style prevailed

throughout the late-Georgian period, dominated by Robert Adam and Sir William

Chambers. The style was inspired by Greek and Roman architecture and the newly

excavated ruins of Pompeii and Herculaneum.

Architectural features became more delicate, and paint colours were used to highlight

plasterwork, with mouldings painted white on a darker ground. Wooden panelling was

replaced with plaster walls and a dado rail that were painted or covered with fabrics

above the dado. Silks, damasks and velvets or flock wallpapers were used in grander

houses, with cotton used in more modest houses.

Finely engraved French wine glass

Drawing room porcelain urn

Left: Many existing buildings were remodelled in the Empire period, and their decorations were changed. The overall style is lighter and more flowing than Palladian, with the emphasis on delicate plasterwork and details, such as anthemions, honeysuckles, swags and husks, which were often placed on top of Neo-Classical columns.

Left: Wallpapers became readily available by the late eighteenth century. Designs reflected the popular Etruscan style, and floral and naturalistic motifs were also popular. French-style gilded furniture appeared as occasional chairs and consoles.

Mahogany was used mostly for furniture, but satinwood was popular for delicate

designs, with intricate inlay and painted flowers and swag motifs. Built-in furniture was

also in vogue, following the forms or curved or oval rooms, or built into specially

designed, symmetrical niches with as much detail as the rest of the room.

Pairs of curtains replaced festoon blinds, and were often hung from a carved

and gilded pelmet designed by the architect. Fabrics were light, with plain silks

and printed chintzes and cottons replacing heavy wools, velvets and damasks.

In the Regency period, emphasis was placed on comfort and practicality, and

architecture returned to a more simple form of Greek revival. There was less formality

to Regency houses, with painted stucco, asymmetrical façades that incorporated bow

and long, full-height windows, and balconies with metalwork details.

Interiors had strong reeded mouldings, plain wall surfaces and ceilings, bold colours

and Greco-Roman and Egyptian motifs as accents. Room colours were selected

primarily with regard to their use and aspect, with darker colours preferred for dining

rooms and libraries, and paler colours for bedrooms. Furniture was placed in the centre

of rooms and around the fireplace; satinwood was used for fine, delicate pieces, and

rosewood for larger items.

Upholstered Empire-style chair

Right: Influenced by French design, festooned and swagged bed hangings echoed the use of fabrics on walls and in tent rooms. Regency bedrooms tended to have floral designs, birds or toile de Jouy on damask, moiré and silks, as well as printed cotton and chintzes.

Heraldic wall frieze

FEDERAL STYLE

It was not until the 1790s that the Neo-Classical style, known in America as Federal – after the new post-Revolution government – began to be seen across the east and south. Houses became lighter and more elegant, with higher ceilings and taller windows, and the Dutch-style pitched roof was replaced by a lower, flatter style, often partly concealed by a balustrade. Porticoes and doors with fanlights were typical, while shutters remained a prominent feature of the American house. The era saw an influx of qualified architects, such as Charles Bulfinch, Samuel McIntyre and John McComb, who practised in different parts of the country and were responsible for the remodelling of many houses.

Interior architectural details were characterized by simple lines, elegant curves and symmetry, and tended to be consistent throughout one room, with the same kind of ornamentation used for all features. Motifs were influenced by Greek and Roman styles, and the eagle was popular as a symbol of Federal America. Simultaneously, fashions moved toward a Classical revival and Palladian works. Houses of this style

Left: Printed cotton upholstery, native American woods and furniture placed in the centre of the room are typical features of this Federal drawing room.

Right: Pineapple roof detail and swagged drawing-room urn

were more robust in stature than Neo-Classical ones, with the emphasis placed on form rather than detail; typical features included round or lunette windows, rectangular fanlights and Greek-style porticoes of one or two storeys.

Interior furnishings were relatively simple early on, with plain painted walls or faux finishes and stencils. Panelling fell out of fashion, and wallpapers came into mass use. Many windows had internal shutters, so window treatments were often purely decorative. Pelmets, swags and tails trimmed with elaborate fringes and draped over poles were more common than heavy curtains. Muslin or light sheers were the favoured window fabrics, especially in the hot and humid South.

Right: High ceilings and tall, undecorated windows give many Federal houses a feeling of light and airiness.

Below left: The Classical influence could be more restrained in its effect than in England, with quiet archways and columns setting the style.

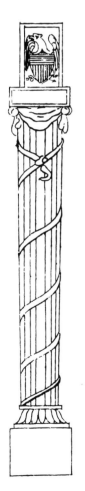

Heraldic column for doorway

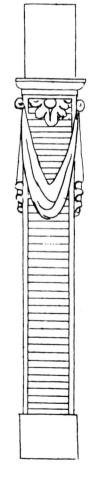

Carved fireplace column

VICTORIAN STYLE

The Victorian era was hugely eclectic in terms of interior design, with a large variety of historical stylings introduced simultaneously: Gothic, Neo-Rococo and Neo-Jacobean, as well as Scottish Baronial and Moorish. More houses were solidly built, and a middle-class terraced house might have three or four floors, with a central or side staircase and two main rooms on each floor. Toward the end of the era there was also a revival of the delicate, refined Queen Anne style, and brick terraced houses replaced the heavier buildings.

Modern conveniences were installed. More rooms had fireplaces fitted with cast-iron grates for burning coal, and gas lamps were more commonly found than candles. Water closets and fitted bathtubs were introduced as water could be pumped to upper floors.

Carved brass doorknocker

Left: Victorian drawing rooms were richly decorated, with painted or papered walls and carved stone, wood or marble fireplaces. Large rooms often had an ecclesiastical feel, influenced by architect Pugin's Gothic-Revival style

Below left: Mahogany or oak were the favoured woods for panelling and larger furniture pieces. Graining, marbling or staining in dark colours were used to replicate this in more modest houses.

Button-upholstered chair

In the main entrance hall and staircase, ceilings were high with deep cornices, and
heavy wood panelling was combined with dark patterned wallpaper to produce a rich
effect. Staircases were normally of dark wood with cast-iron or woodturned balusters,
with a large newel post at the base and a carpet or matting runner up the main flight.
Encaustic floor tiles replaced stone in entrance halls and porches. Walls were divided
into three sections with a dado rail and frieze or picture rail; the upper section was often
wallpapered with a flock paper or large design. There was also a trend to paint ceilings in
a colour and to incorporate a frieze.

Soft furnishings were lush and luxurious, and with the introduction of sophisticated
printing techniques, synthetic dyes and design inspiration, there was a mass of choice to
suit all tastes. Fabric was used as curtains and throws, and as room dividers. New
furniture materials were used, such as cast iron for table or chair legs; iron bedsteads
were also popular, often painted or finished in polished brass. Papier-mâché was used for
occasional pieces of furniture and objects such as trays and boxes, painted with foliage or
inlaid with mother-of-pearl.

Gas-lamp or candle-holder

Right: No Victorian drawing
room was complete without a
mass of accessories. Much
Victorian furniture is robust
and bulbous, to suit the style
of the ornaments and rooms.

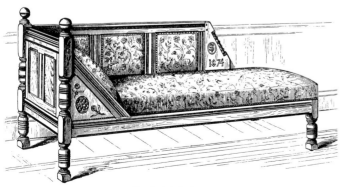

Panelled chaise longue

ARTS AND CRAFTS STYLE

The Arts and Crafts movement evolved as a reaction to revolt against the excesses and

eclecticism of the Victorian era. There was a return to quality, fine craftsmanship and a

desire to express new ideas and individualism. William Morris, the chief English

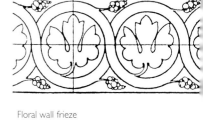

Floral wall frieze

exponent, was responsible for the initiation of the movement through the 1860s

onward, but it was the writings of John Ruskin that made a new generation of artists

and designers aware of the qualities of the Medieval period and the importance of

honesty in craftsmanship.

Architects such as the London-based Philip Webb looked to a simple, vernacular

style of architecture, with asymmetrical design, exposed brickwork and simple

furnishings. Low-level wainscoting, normally made of tongue-and-groove boards, was

reintroduced, and the walls above were generally wallpapered up to a picture rail, often

used to display decorative plates. Woodwork was either varnished or painted a light

colour, in particular green, or a shade that would enhance the wallpaper.

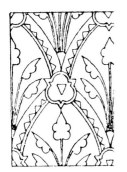

Printed wallpaper design

At the same time another style was emerging: the Aesthetic movement embodied the

desire for lighter, refined design and beautiful taste. Houses were largely built of brick,

with asymmetrical gables and tall, narrow leaded windows. The interiors were

influenced by Pre-Raphaelite paintings and Japanese designs, with a combination of

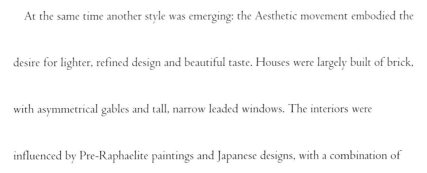

Left: The Gothic revival meets the Arts and Crafts style in its use of stained and
coloured glass in huge, impressive picture windows.

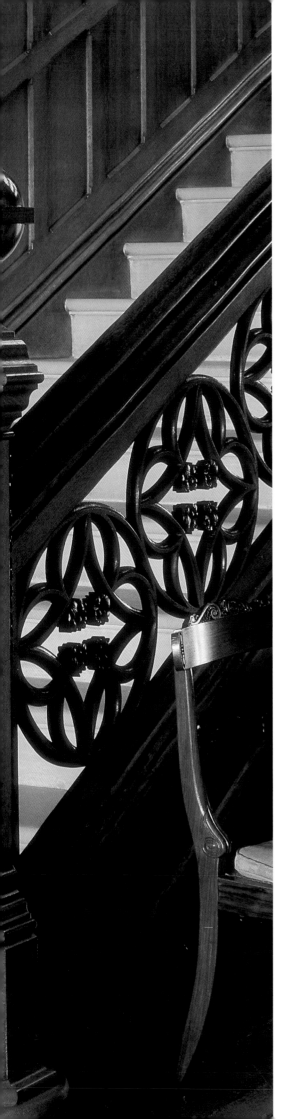

soft, subtle colours and oriental-inspired fabric designs, furniture and *objets d'art*.

Other influential architects and designers of the period in Britain were Charles Voysey and Sir Edwin Lutyens. Voysey loved detail and, like Robert Adam in the Neo-Classical era, designed every detail of a room, including all the furnishings and accessories. In contrast to Adam, however, his designs were very simple and architecturally sparse, while his fabrics and wallpapers were influenced by nature, using stylized flowers, foliage and animals. Lutyens's influence was seen toward the end of the period; he introduced partially timbered houses.

Curtains were lightweight and made from printed cotton or chintz, linens and muslins, and were hung on wooden or brass poles. Handwoven and embroidered fabrics were also extremely popular, with a new generation of women on both sides of the Atlantic producing beautiful designs, mostly used for bedspreads, throws and cushions.

By 1870 Queen Anne style had become popular in America, and led to the development of a truly American Arts and Crafts movement. This was largely influenced by Gustav Stickley's publication *The Craftsman*, and brothers Henry and Charles Greene, who produced spacious open-plan houses, forerunners to the designs of Frank Lloyd Wright.

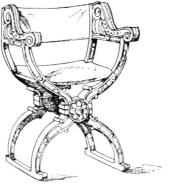

Eastern-style throne chair

Right: Arts and Crafts furniture was strikingly simple, handmade with traditional techniques and preferably naturally aged woods such as oak. Handmade rugs were another popular feature.

THE HOUSES TODAY

Today, it is really unusual to find an old, period house that has survived

intact and untouched by progress since it was built – and the few houses

of this kind that do ever appear on the market are eagerly snapped up.

However, aged houses which have been adapted and improved are almost

always more comfortable than a fully original one, and boast no less character

and style. It is perfectly acceptable to decorate and furnish your house with the best

and most appropriate period furniture from the various centuries the house embodies,

providing always that there is a unity of feel and that the internal architecture of the

house echoes the style of your choice.

Left: This Victorian Jacobean-style hall and staircase area was built with three-quarter-height
polished oak panelling and staircase. A strapwork ceiling adds architectural emphasis, and the
two-tone damask-design wallpaper provides warmth above the panelling and above the stair,
without being too busy to hang pictures on.

HALLS

The hall and its use have changed and evolved over the centuries. From the Medieval

period through to the Georgian one, the hall was used for a variety of functions, from

eating and entertaining to family gatherings and even sleeping. Decoration was sparse

and simple, with white or stonewashed walls, which were sometimes painted as stone

blocks – a style that has been revived in recent times.

During the seventeenth and eighteenth centuries, as families now ate in the relative

privacy of a separate room or parlour, the hall became more of a vestibule or waiting

room. In contrast to the splendour of Baroque and Rococo ornamentation that might

prevail in the rest of the public rooms in the house, it was a sparsely furnished area,

often with little more than a couple of high-backed or side chairs or benches where

guests would wait for a short time before being escorted by servants to the main areas.

The emphasis was placed on architectural details, with the fireplace – now placed at one

end of the room, instead of in the centre, as previously – and perhaps the staircase

forming the focal points.

Today, halls are likely to be treated and furnished as rooms to use and to live in, and

quite often have a dual purpose, perhaps for dining in, as in the original usage, for

taking tea in, or even as an extra reading room or study. In terraced houses that may

have a hall that is little more than a corridor, a hall-cum-dining room or study can be

created by enlarging the opening and putting in double doors, or by knocking down the

entire wall and inserting a supporting beam. In larger houses, there may be the luxury of

Right: The area shown here is part of a hall in a house in Wales that dates back to Tudor times and the sixteenth century. The original oak beams form a strong architectural feature throughout the house, and although the hall space is small, it is furnished as a room, using period oak furniture that is suitable both for the style and age of the house, and for its proportions and scale.

an outer hall or porch, which gives you more freedom to furnish the hall as an

additional drawing room or dining area.

While halls have to be practical, being the first point of entry from the outside, they

should also be warm and inviting. Hard floor surfaces, such as stone, tiles or wood, are

more suitable than wall-to-wall carpeting, and you can use rugs to help soften the

appearance and absorb excess noise.

I try to treat halls or even corridors, however small, like a room with its own merits

and possibilities, making sure that the emphasis is placed on practicality and warmth.

Bare, painted walls are cold and uninviting, so I like to utilize either a wallpaper or

decorative paint finish. If, as is often the case, the staircase runs directly off the hall,

installing a dado rail allows you to use a combination of finishes, for instance a durable

paint that can be wiped down below the rail, and wallpaper above. Alternatively, you

could use a variety of paint finishes, perhaps incorporating *trompe l'oeil*; paint helps to

protect the walls from small fingers and damage from items being carried up and down

the hall and staircase.

Halls can be architectural and have focal points. If there is no fireplace in situ, you

Right: This eighteenth-century Georgian hall is very architectural in its overall design, and the beautiful
panelling and plasterwork ceiling provide an elegant ambience. The marble-topped console table is flanked
by the two chairs forming a focal point on one wall, and the colourful rug is a source of warmth; it also
assists with absorbing the sound and possible echoes that can result from bare wooden floorboards.

can consider creating a niche to display a piece of furniture and a painting, or an archway flanked with columns and pilasters. Obviously the size and proportions of your hall influence what you do, but don't be put off just because the space may seem small and insignificant – first impressions count for a lot!

Give thought to the lighting in a hall. This needs to be in keeping with the overall atmosphere, and I favour traditional brass lanterns and chandeliers over downlighters, combined with lamps if there is space, and wall sconces or picture lights.

Below: The hall and staircase of this country farmhouse show features typical of the Victorian period, such as the painted balusters combined with a polished wooden handrail, and the patterned stair runner fixed with brass stair rods. The polished oak floorboards act as a practical finish, while the rich patina from the wood furniture gives a feeling of warmth.

Right: Personal possessions and *objets d'art* provide a lived-in and welcoming feel anywhere, so long as they are positioned with care. The space under the stairs in the farmhouse is cleverly designed to maximize its storage potential, while preserving space to display the vintage pram and the antique oak chest that acts as a central log basket.

DRAWING ROOMS

Drawing rooms as we know them developed in the Empire and Colonial periods in the eighteenth century, and were then largely considered to be 'feminine' rooms, an area where the ladies would invite their guests to take tea and play cards or sew. In the evenings, a drawing room was one to which women could 'withdraw' after dinner, while the men stayed in the dining room or retreated to the masculine environment of the library, study or smoking room.

In particularly grand houses, the drawing room was frequently situated on the first floor or *piano nobile*. There might also be a separate 'saloon', which was then used as the formal room for entertaining guests and visitors; as in previous times, the saloon was hung with fabrics and woven tapestries and the furniture was placed sparsely around the room, while the less formal drawing room had groups of furniture and perhaps double-hung pictures. Generally speaking, today's drawing rooms tend to be grander rooms than sitting rooms, and if both are present in the same house, drawing rooms are the ones used for entertaining.

Left: This is the 'new' part of a double drawing room, which is an extension from an original Victorian room with a Georgian feel. The newly purchased eighteenth-century fireplace is of a similar type to that in the original part, while the modern cornices are typical of Empire style. The room has two seating areas, one around the fireplace, using comfortable upholstered pieces, and the other in the bay window, which uses French gilt furniture. The decoration is based around the reproduction Aubusson rugs.

Furnishings in a drawing room have always tended to be grander than those of a morning room or sitting room, and the key to success in modern times is to strike a balance between formal elegance and the kind of comfortable, relaxed atmosphere that has become the norm for most people today. In my view, drawing rooms should be kept as clear as possible of modern, incongruous televisions, computers and so on; along with stereo systems, these can be discreetly hidden in pieces of furniture or custom-made joinery, or even behind screens.

In the early days of the drawing room as a separate entity, furniture would be placed around the perimeter of the room, with small groups of upright chairs in the centre, but as the eighteenth century progressed and gave way to the Victorian era, it brought the introduction of deep upholstered pieces and elaborate window treatments, which evoked a more comfortable feeling.

One point worth remembering is that, as the formal face of the house, the drawing room of the later eighteenth and nineteenth centuries would be used as a repository of furnishings and accessories – the sheer number of surfaces and objects that covered every part of them in a typical middle-class Victorian drawing room seems incredible

Left: The use of earthy colours and the large stone flagstones unite the various uses of this Medieval-style great hall, now part-drawing room and part-dining room. The overall effect is one of light and space, even with a fair amount of furnishings and drapery present. The large hanging drapes also serve to cut down on the inevitable noise that results in a high, open room.

today, now that we no longer have a surplus of easily available servants to clean and care

for everything. If you plan to recreate these eras faithfully in each detail, you must also

be prepared to make the inevitable effort to care for it. In larger houses, of course, the

same amount of possessions can be spread out further, thus avoiding the possibility of

clutter and overcrowding.

In the seventeenth century the use of strong colours and fabrics became popular, with

silk damask and velvets among the most preferred for hangings. Matching fabrics were

used for chair covers and curtains, with the effect of bringing unity to the furnishings.

Rich crimson colours were often installed as a good background for paintings and other

objets d'art purchased on the Grand Tour, which was regarded as an integral part of

finishing a gentleman's education. This new custom of bringing back cultural artifacts

that had been personally collected also marked a shift in emphasis: from the influence

of designers and architects, who would furnish a room from ceiling to floor, to a less

heterogenous, more personal expression of taste. Fabric wall hangings later gave way to

wallpaper, sometimes block-printed, and plain painted walls.

The style of curtains evolved from simply hanging them from iron rods to more

elaborate styles, initially influenced by French fashions. Many large windows were

Right: In older houses, where rooms may lead off one another and not always off a main corridor or hall,
give thought to the views from room to room. A small sitting room that leads off a dark library or study
can mark a change in room usage, and a cosy window seat suggests informality and personal use, as
against the formality of more public spaces.

adorned by two sets of curtains: lightweight undercurtains of muslin or voile, and fixed outer curtains in brilliantly coloured, rich, heavyweight fabrics, which were frequently trimmed with tassels, fringes and cords. Palladian rooms with high ceilings and elegant windows would have festoons that were pulled up on drawstrings and had the advantage of not interfering with the architectural details of the window frames or shutters.

Even though there are no longer any hard and fast formal rules, the placing of furniture in such a public room is important, and a number of separate seating areas may be required, depending on the size and layout of the room. Symmetrical positioning may also be an important factor in a formal room, especially if there is a central fireplace that forms the focal point and is a natural area for seating.

Bay or bow windows are perfect for use as one of the individual seating areas mentioned above, and by installing window seats you can make good use of the space while still enjoying the view. This is also an area where I like to install a permanent card table with chairs – ideal for a game of cards or a jigsaw puzzle, for instance – or, as an alternative, a pretty desk for the use of guests.

The style of furniture should be selected according to the period of the house, and should be of that period itself if possible. Many eighteenth- and nineteenth-century houses were almost entirely furnished with pieces imported from France, Italy, Holland and so on, and so it is quite acceptable, and even authentic, to use a combination of furniture. There is no shortage of drawing-room furniture of most periods and styles, both authentic and accurate reproductions.

Left: The colour scheme here is typical of the Federal era, with a butter-yellow panelled wall against white columns, ceiling and imposing, Neo-Classical fireplace. While not original, the comfortable armchairs lend a touch of luxury to the slightly austere surroundings.

This view of the double drawing room on page 58 shows the damask-covered walls. The fabric was specially woven for the room, and is used in combination with plain silk for the curtains – a treatment typical of eighteenth-century styles. The room evokes balance, harmony and symmetry, with the fireplace forming the focal point and the furniture carefully placed in relation to it. Because suitable period pieces proved hard to find, the custom-made, gilded wooden consoles were hand carved in the appropriate styles.

Below and right: Chinoiserie style, popular in the latter part of the eighteenth century, is often thought of as too ornate for a contemporary interior – possibly because some surviving original examples (such as England's Brighton Pavilion) tend toward this end of the spectrum. This London drawing room, however, uses the Chinese influences to create a haven of elegance and serenity. The walls are hand-painted and are reminiscent of an eighteenth-century parlour, while the soft gold-and-ochre hues and monochromatic colour scheme throughout the room provide a warm and welcoming ambience. The theme of Chinoiserie is repeated in the delicate lacquered tables.

Right: This is another view of the drawing room on page 64, and shows the yellow walls broken only by a large, plain mirror above a dark sideboard. The pretty, delicate floral designs on the central couch contrast with the tree-in-pot motif on the cushion on the right-hand chair. This was a favourite naïve image, often worked in cross stitch by the women of the house.

70

Good-quality contemporary pieces can also work well, in particular for supplying furniture that was not around at the time when the house was built, such as coffee tables, nests of tables, television cabinets and so on. If you go down this route, make sure from the start that the craftsmanship and finish are top-quality and in keeping with what you wish to achieve. Be aware in addition that reproduction leather stuffed chairs and sofas can look very new and out of place in a period drawing room, and it is worth making the effort to seek out companies that specialize in furniture that doesn't need decades of wear before it fits.

Below: The Neo-Classical influence is unmistakable here, with the elaborate painted fireplace, gilded mirror surround and three urns on the mantelpiece designed in the Greek style. The shelves in the alcoves on either side are a cross between fitted cupboards and a library, while the pale painted panels are warmed by the yellow of the wall sconces.

Right: The overwhelming impression in this Empire drawing room is of light, with no curtains or blinds on the long windows, but shutters that can be closed from the outside. The rich red of the walls is echoed in the upholstery scheme, and the window seat is high enough to allow the view outside to be seen in comfort.

If you feel that your drawing room lacks the finesse of architectural details, you can quite easily overcome this and enrich the surroundings by adding a decent plaster cornice, and perhaps a dado rail or panel moulding. Even small details, such as the size and finish of the architraves and skirtings, can make a noticeable difference, so it is important not to do too much to a room at once.

On the other hand, if you already have a beautiful period drawing room with exquisite architectural detail, make sure that the decoration and furnishings are not so elaborate that they detract from the original built-in character of the room. Sometimes, for example, I find it is better to leave an original window untreated, so that it can enhance fine mouldings and shutters.

Lighting in drawing rooms should be largely atmospheric, but never dull. Oil lamps were improved throughout the later eighteenth and early nineteenth centuries, and could be made to burn brightly or subtly, depending on the occasion. To reproduce their effects, use mainly table lamps to provide illumination. A grand drawing room with a high ceiling can benefit from one or more pendant crystal or brass chandeliers, perhaps with matching wall sconces.

In general, paintings and other artwork on the walls should be lit by discreet picture lights attached to the picture frame; alternatively, if you are able to plan your lighting before rebuilding a ceiling, you can inset tiny angled, pinpoint spotlights. From the Baroque era on, most grand fireplaces had equally grand and often ornate mirrors above them; in addition to their decorative use, the mirrors also reflected central

Left: This typical Victorian drawing room includes a dominant fireplace which is original to the room. The wood panelling is also authentic, and the use of soft gold paint helps it to blend in harmoniously with the furnishings, which feature period-style fringes and tassels. The patterned carpet was specially woven, and the Italian leather screen conceals a large television set.

pendant lighting, thus increasing the illumination. Some wall sconces would have polished metal surfaces placed between them in the wall, to make maximum use of the available light sources for reading or playing card games.

Wooden and parquet floors look at their best when they are dark, rather than light, and polished, which both adds warmth and colour and offsets formality. Rugs should be carefully chosen to be in harmony with the overall colour scheme, perhaps echoing any patterning on fabrics, and can be one large one or a series of small ones; Persian and Middle Eastern rugs have been popular choices since the eighteenth century, and simple handwoven rugs work well in Colonial drawing rooms.

Above left: Adding a simple vase of flowers can turn a plain window alcove into a delightful study in its own right.

Left and right: These two views of an Empire-style drawing room show the dramatic design possibilities provided by a large bay window. With a window seat along its length, and a large blind at the top, it is framed by a characteristic yellow pelmet and curtains, whose colour is carried onto the settee and armchairs. All the accessories blend in harmoniously with, and complement this light, airy colour scheme.

LIBRARIES AND STUDIES

Traditionally masculine rooms, libraries and studies developed during the eighteenth century to store not only a well-read gentleman's books, but also artifacts acquired from his travels through Europe on the Grand Tour. The rooms were frequently panelled, with a variety of styles and finishes. Earlier rooms had full-height, painted panelling divided by a dado rail. The walls often incorporated bookcases, which were treated as part of the room, and architectural details with Classical motifs, such as egg and dart, Greek key and pilasters. In grander houses, the wood would be polished mahogany, walnut or oak, either full-height or below the dado only, combined with fabric, wallpaper or paint above. Floors were wooden parquet or plank in oak or pine; area rugs were not used until the late eighteenth century.

If creating a library today from scratch, a painted, panelled room that incorporates bookcases should be cheaper than polished wood. However, a polished wood finish such as mahogany will evoke a rich, masculine look. To enhance design and detail, you can paint the panels in three tones of one colour, or leave the mouldings white. Bookcases should look like a piece of furniture and become an architectural feature, rather than a boring row of shelves. The use of different shapes and sizes within one room, such as a breakfront unit with a central pediment, adds interest.

Left: In this early-eighteenth-century painted study, the walls and details have been painted in one shade, typical of the period. On the narrow panels the ornamental plates allow the painting over the fireplace to become the focal point of the room. The white blinds cut out harmful sun rays and protect the furniture.

Right: This large, grand Victorian library evokes a strong, masculine, yet welcoming atmosphere. The Gothic influence, typical of the era, is particularly apparent in the panelled ceiling and large built-in unit that incorporates the fireplace. Here, all the bookcases are built-in on the gallery level, and the larger books are displayed on large library tables below. The combination of the polished wood architectural details and the green-painted walls provides a rich and distinctive ambience.

Below: Leatherbound books look much more appealing and authentic in library bookcases than dog-eared paperbacks. If you cannot afford the genuine article, reproduction books can be bought by the yard and offer a good alternative. Break up a run of books with a sculpture, small painting, photograph frame or wooden box.

Left: Using a light, clouded aubergine to rag-roll plum-coloured walls provides a wonderful background colour. The oak plank floor adds richness, and the white skirting forms a defined break between the two. Leather wing chairs are typical library pieces: try to use antique or antiqued leather.

Right: This contemporary library is used for displaying artifacts, such as the earthenware urns, acquired on travels. Oak furniture is more suitable than mahogany in a farmhouse, and the wool paisley of the curtains adds warmth — without being too busy — while maintaining the masculine feel.

DINING ROOMS

Dining rooms as we know them today did not come into existence until the eighteenth century, when the desire to entertain on a grand scale became paramount. During the Medieval period, all family dining and entertaining took place in the hall or great hall, but as buildings evolved along with the desire for greater comfort and privacy, informal family dining moved to the parlour, a sort of morning room, or in grander houses to the chamber, an anteroom of the great chamber or master bedroom. A legacy of this can be found in some stately homes, where keeping the food warm during the long journey from the kitchen to the table – sometimes on a different storey – became a test of skill in itself.

Early dining rooms were not permanently furnished, and trestle-type tables, chairs and benches may have been placed around the perimeter of the room, or dining tables may have been especially brought in and set up, then cleared away again at the end of the meal or occasion.

Large dining tables and upholstered chairs became popular in the mid-eighteenth century, and became permanent features in the dining room before the end of the century. Mahogany imported from Honduras was the favoured wood, with walnut and

Left: This Jacobean-style Victorian dining room was originally a very plain room with no architectural features. The strapwork ceiling, dado rail and panel moulding were all added to give a more authentic feel. The walls are stippled in a honey colour, and the mouldings have been wiped so as not to be bright white. The dining table is antique, but the reproduction chairs were specially commissioned for the room, the design being taken from an original Irish chair.

rosewood being used for smaller pieces. Sideboards incorporated urns that held water

for washing glasses and cutlery, and other practical pieces of furniture, such as wine

coolers, soon developed; these were often designed specifically by the architect to fit

into an alcove or niche.

At this time dining rooms tended to be quite masculine rooms, with the emphasis

being placed on hunting or drinking themes, which were depicted in architectural

details, such as grapes and vines as features on ceiling mouldings, or horns and masks

incorporated in a fireplace frieze. It was unusual for dining rooms of this time to be

curtained – carved shutters were the favoured option. The panelled walls in the Rococo

period might be painted white and gold, and a little later, in the Adam brothers'

Georgian era, softer and paler colours came into popularity.

Rather like libraries and studies, in general late-eighteenth- and nineteenth-century

dining rooms reverted to being dark, again emphasizing the masculine feel, but also

bringing warmth to the ambience. Because rooms were lit only by candlelight until the

latter part of the nineteenth century, when first gas lighting and then electric

lighting became widespread, dark, warm colours were the preferred option and provided

a strong background for mirrors, oil paintings and family portraits.

Today, the formal dining room has lost much of its original appeal and can be rather

a wasted room, often used little more then a few times a year for family gatherings,

holidays and the odd dinner party. Our hectic lifestyles and the lack of inexpensive and

Right: This Colonial kitchen features a large table and fitted wall cupboards of native American wood, and the table is laid with characteristic blue-and-white crockery and brass candlesticks.

Left: This Federal dining room
shows some of the changes
that had come about since the
Colonial room on page 87.
These include: striped drab
wallpaper above a dado rail
replacing panelling; a plaster
ceiling; an inlaid table and chairs
with padded seats; and a glass
chandelier. The swags and
pelmet allow maximum light to
come in from the glass-
panelled doors and windows.

easily obtained domestic help have led us to adopt the originally American style of one-

room living, with the dining room now incorporating a kitchen, an eating area and

often an area for sitting and relaxation.

Undoubtedly, this modern style of living is more convenient when one has to act as

cook, cleaner, mother or father, wife or husband, and host or hostess all at the same

time. However, if there is the luxury of space available, I particularly enjoy the elegant

and romantic atmosphere of a formal dining room and the sight of a beautiful table

laden with exquisite accessories.

In smaller town or city houses, it is practical and quite acceptable to have either a

dining area in a larger sitting room or a dining room that doubles up as another room,

Right: This shows the view from the main hall into the dining room, which can be shut off with the double pocket doors; however, they are mostly left open to give a vista and more daylight to the hall. The two strapwork ceilings are of similar design, although that of the dining room is purposely more elaborate.

Right: Fireplaces always create a focal point, and this restored original, beautifully carved pine mantelpiece is a typical eighteenth-century design, depicting the drinking motifs of grapes, vine leaves and urn. In this dining room, right, a picture hangs over the mantelpiece, but often mirrors would be used to help reflect the candlelight.

Above left: A plate cupboard is cleverly concealed within the wall panelling. It is both practical and decorative, as the door can be left open to display plates.

Below left: Chenille curtains break up the run of wood panelling. When not in use, extra chairs are placed around the perimeter of the room.

Right: The panelling in this room is new, with the design copied from existing examples in the hall. Speakers are concealed in two upper panels and painted in with the woodwork. The court cupboard and chairs are antique, but the table is new: round tables with central pedestals were not typical of the Jacobean period, but gate-leg tables can be awkward to sit at. The limestone floor is covered with a bound sisal rug.

Left: This simple, elegant panelled dining room is typical of an early-eighteenth-century parlour, used for family dining. The furniture is all mahogany, which is in keeping with the style and period of the room, and a white linen damask tablecloth has been used here, rather than place mats. The black-and-white engravings are in keeping with the period and do not detract from the simplicity of the room, where even the window is left undressed and unornamented. The working shutters can be closed at night.

95

such as a hall or study. I find bookcases in a dining room rather an appealing decorative feature, especially when, in early houses, they are adorned with a collection of porcelain, glass or silver, or pewter and brass.

Because a formal dining room of this kind tends to be predominantly used at night or on special occasions, it is the one room where you can consistently afford to be bold and adventurous in your choice of decoration. My favourites are various shades of reds, crimsons, coral or rich blues – dark greens can be a bit sombre for large formal rooms and are perhaps better for a more informal farmhouse dining room. For lighter, more daytime dining rooms I also like to use the typical Adam colours of turquoise, yellow and light green.

How you decorate will depend on the scale and proportions of your dining room. If you have a high ceiling, it may prove advantageous to install a dado rail and split the wall surface into two, in order to combine different wall finishes: fabric, wallpaper or paint above, combined with plain paint, panelling or a faux effect, such as marblized

Left: The strong, oxblood-red painted walls are typical of a Victorian dining room, and the contrasting off-white of the arch and wall below the dado is very striking. The original oak plank floor is covered with a rather threadbare rug, which adds character to the room. The robust buttoned-leather chairs with carved turned legs are typical of the period, and the sideboard is used to display ornaments and flowers.

Top right: As an alternative to using a lace mat or cloth to keep the table surface unmarked, a carved wooden vase or pot stand of matching wood is used.

Middle right: The individual lights feature silhouetted fairies, and the shape of the lightshades directs a pool of warm light onto the polished table top.

Bottom right: Victorian attention to each detail of the dining table is apparent in these handmade glasses with their golden settings.

walls. Fabric has the advantage of acting as a sound absorber and enhancing acoustics,

but the disadvantage of harbouring food and tobacco smells.

Whatever the colour scheme you adopt, candlelight always brings atmosphere to

dining rooms, with a soft, flickering glow that enhances the wall and furniture colours.

You have the choice of using either original or reproduction candlesticks or candelabra

on the table, on the sideboard or freestanding on the floor, while chandeliers and wall

sconces offer further opportunities.

Below and opposite: This Gothic-revival Victorian dining room is very warm, with a central stone 'heraldic' fireplace, red-leather buttoned chairs and full-length polished panelling. The deep-relief plasterwork ceiling has a red base colour, with blue and gold used to pick out the prominent areas.

BEDROOMS

Over the centuries the bedroom has undergone quite a radical change in its use. It has

become a particularly personal space, a room to retreat to, in which one can seek and

find privacy and tranquillity. In earlier centuries this was certainly not the case, and, up

until the mid-sixteenth century, separate bedchambers did not exist. In Medieval times

sleeping areas were communal ones, with most people sleeping on beds of straw or

horsehair or straw mattresses placed on the ground.

Right: This Baroque bedroom, with its painted panelling and tapestry wall hangings, is dominated by the
four-poster bed completely covered in hangings. The low barley-twist turned oak chair is pushed back
against the wall, adding to the impression of spaciousness in what is not a hugely tall room.

Below: The heavy gold-embroidered floral motifs on the bed hangings match those on the dark blue velvet
bedspread. The effect is of luxurious formality, if not easy or comfortable, aided by the dark red of the
tapestry work above the bedhead.

Beds were very important status symbols and were the possessions of only the most

wealthy members of society. Four-posters were the most common type and were

designed for their practicality; the bed was the only piece of furniture found at that

time that was dressed with fabric, in order both to provide privacy and to protect the

occupants from draughts.

Early four-poster beds were simple in design and ornamentation, and were almost

invariably made of oak, while the draperies were made from wool or linen and were

hung from metal rods. It was only in the eighteenth century, when more and more

fabrics were being produced and exported and imported, that bed treatments became

more lavish and elaborate.

In larger houses the main bedroom or great chamber would have been located on the

first floor or *piano nobile*, the same floor as the rooms that were used for entertaining.

The other, lesser bedrooms were on the next level, while the attic space was reserved

for servants. It was not uncommon at this time for a husband and wife to have separate

bedrooms, as well as a private sitting room attached to one or the other, where they

could take their meals in private.

Right: As on the previous pages, a four-poster bed dominates its surroundings, but in this Federal bedroom
the result is lighter and more colourful. The blue of the antique bedspread is carried over to the curtains,
and also features in the shaped patterns on the bed hangings. The fireplace is a modest brick one, and the
panelling is light in colour, allowing the small portraits to be seen in context.

The Early Georgian era of the eighteenth century saw the first major growth in

purely speculative building, to cope both with an increase in population and with a great

influx into cities and towns. Brick-built terraced houses became home to many, and the

way in which they were built and architecturally decorated was subject for the first time

to governmental acts. This meant that the main bedrooms were 'light' – that is,

provided with one or more windows – while those of servants, which often led off the

main bedrooms, were 'dark' and without a window.

The trend thus begun has been the style ever since, and in many houses and

apartments today, especially in cities where space may be at a premium, bedrooms tend

Right: Even today, when a bedroom is regarded as more of a private refuge from the world outside, there is plenty of scope to use accessories and furnishings to make a personal statement to the world. Something as simple as not putting away bedlinen and covers – whether antique or modern reproduction – but showing them neatly folded, can set off a room to perfection – as well as being a fine napping place for pets.

Right: This pretty Victorian-style bedroom uses the theme of red, pink and white throughout, from the bedhead down through the cushions to the bedspread; it is carried on to the throw over the bedside table. If you decide to follow the Victorian style of grouping many pictures on the walls, make sure that the background colour is sympathetic and does not impose – here, the different styles, colours and shapes of frames create a unity together.

Above: The spray of fresh flowers is echoed in the motif on the jug and bowl.

Below left: Antique bed linen enhances any bed, and these old Welsh quilts make very fine throws at the end of a bed or on a chaise.

Below centre: This dressing table is dressed with antique crystal and silver accessories, and a hand-crocheted lace mat.

to be small in proportion and therefore difficult to furnish with much flair, particularly when the bed is forced to become the focal point in the room. By over-dressing a bed in a small room with elaborate bed draperies, or by installing a four-poster where space does not really allow it, the room can become very claustrophobic and have the opposite of a calming atmosphere – these treatments and methods of furnishing should be reserved for larger town- or country-house bedrooms.

Personally, I prefer to keep all built-in wardrobes for clothes out of the bedroom and instead, if space permits, keep garments in a separate dressing room or walk-in cupboard, as was the case with practically all the bedrooms in the eras covered by this book; the bathroom is not an ideal solution, however, as it is too damp for clothes storage. For a medium-to-small-size bedroom, authentic or good reproduction chests of drawers and tallboys are plentiful and not too expensive.

Below right: It is relaxing to have a small sofa, chaise or armchair in the bedroom. Corners are often wasted spaces, so this love seat, covered with a pretty quilt, is an ideal solution.

Right: Traditional floral chintz was the starting point for the decoration of this bedroom, and the wall colour was taken from the fabric. The strong colour of the walls makes the room appear smaller, although, combined with the white paint, it makes for a striking appearance. The iron bed gives the room a Victorian feel.

A working fireplace is wonderful for creating a romantic bedroom, with a couple of cosy armchairs or a chaise longue at the end of the bed. Architectural salvage firms and specialist manufacturers produce a wide variety of fire grates, surrounds and mantelpieces for all periods, and it is worth taking away later covering boards and unblocking chimney flues for the warmth and beauty of a real fire.

My other idea of perfection is to have a window view from the bed – again, this is difficult to achieve in cities unless you have a spectacular loft apartment or a skyscraper

Left: This guest bedroom is large enough to have a king-size bed with a half tester over it to create a focal point. The carved gilt pelmets from which the fabric pelmets hang are new, but the designs were inspired by eighteenth-century originals. The bed is purposely high, in order for the occupants to benefit from the views from the window. The overall effect is of a late-eighteenth-century bedroom.

Below: This serene panelled bedroom is typical of an English country house where the rooms lead into one another, with perhaps the dressing room being next door. Once again the bed is the main feature: a four-poster dressed with old chintz that has been updated and relined at a later stage, a good way to preserve original character in a room. The walls are painted in one pale colour, to give a serene, calm look, and they contrast well with the original mahogany door.

in New York, or a view over a town park or private gardens. Outside town, however,

nothing beats waking up to a beautiful, quiet view of the countryside on a sunny

morning: it instantly puts you in a good frame of mind, and how you place your bed to

catch this is another important factor.

The use of colours in a bedroom is a very personal matter – much more so than in

any other room in the house, it appears – and different people find different colours

peaceful and calm. For instance, I love a blue bedroom. Having had one ever since I was

a child, I have never understood the philosophy that blue should be for a boy and pink

Left: This small lobby provides a little dressing area between a main bedroom and bathroom, and has its own outside staircase leading to the garden. The half-glazed door provides daylight into what could otherwise be a dark area, and a single crewelwork curtain provides privacy at night. The antique painted shelf unit provides useful storage space.

Right: This master bedroom of an old house has purposely been kept simple, as the stunning views from its windows provide the best backdrop. The fabric-covered screen provides some privacy from the dressing area and acts as a draught protector. All the furniture is antique, and the bed is dressed with old linen and Welsh quilts.

for a girl – and certainly not once the child is past the first few weeks of infancy.

Although certain shades of blue can undoubtedly be cold and uninviting,

choosing the right hue – one that is neither too Wedgwood or lilac, nor too

strong and vivid or dominating – can create an immensely serene atmosphere. In

addition, I do not like fussy patterned wallpapers in a bedroom and prefer

instead a small simple design or paint finish, which allows you the option of

having the walls covered with watercolours or pretty floral prints.

While chintz fabric has gone in and out of fashion in many rooms of the

house, the one room where it has always remained popular is a country house

bedroom. Chintz was first manufactured in large quantities and used, along with

toile de Jouy, in eighteenth-century houses. It has been a firm favourite ever since,

meaning that there is a wide choice of colours and patterns available, so you

should not have too much trouble finding something that both suits the room

Left: This blue-and-white country-house bedroom offers a quiet, calm atmosphere, and the
contrasting wood of the bed and bedside tables adds age and warmth. The walls are patterned
and the curtains are almost plain; they are linked in with the walls by their blue-and-cream fringe,
so as not to distract from the view into the garden. The bed is dressed in crisp white antique linen,
which always looks inviting.

Above right: A two-tone blue cotton damask fabric has been used for these curtains, trimmed
with a matching fan edge and fringe for the pelmet.

and is in keeping with the age of the house. Used with thought, chintz can help to create a country-house atmosphere in a town house – but don't let it become too overwhelming or – even with a light design – oppressive.

I think that many people choose pink as the dominant colour in their bedrooms because they feel that pink is a pretty, feminine colour which will reflect warmth and have the effect of bringing the garden indoors. In my view, pink is acceptable in moderation; like all colours, there are hues that work and those that are just too vibrant to be peaceful. Rich, crimson walls are fine for a large room that may need warming up, but for rooms that are naturally bright or light choose a

Below left: This charming corner of a country-house bedroom evokes warmth and calm. It is large enough to incorporate a desk, as well as a seating area in the bay window, and the old hat boxes and antique clothes give a turn-of-the-century feel to the room.

Below: In a room where the window gives onto lovely views, a low carved-oak chest allows the light to flow in unimpeded and is a minor focal point in the bay area.

Right: This pretty, informal country-house bedroom has a neutral look, neither masculine nor feminine. This is largely due to the chintz curtains being balanced by the beige wallpaper; if the walls had been pink, the room would have appeared much more feminine. An antique quilt used as a bedspread is more appealing than a new one, which can appear somewhat hotel-like.

Left: With its large stone fireplace and
exposed antique beams, this guest bedroom
in a country house is naturally inviting; it
requires a simple decorative treatment in
order not to detract from the existing
architectural features. The paisley throws on
the armchair and antique cushions fit in well
with the overall effect.

Right: The small seating area, by the fireplace
and in the corner, makes this bedroom very
cosy, furnished as it is with personal objects
that are significant to the owner. The beams
and rough lime-plastered walls add to the
informality of the room, and the sunlight
streaming in from the window gives a feeling
of serenity and warmth.

Right: The three alcoves in this large bedroom are each used in a very different manner. The one nearest the door is a small library of fitted bookshelves, while the one leading onto the window bay allows light to stream into the room. In between, the large, sumptuous four-poster bed contrasts the green of the fabric by its head with the strong yellow of the walls.

Below: In this guest bedroom, the furnishings also provide a contrast, with the light, solid-wood bedsteads being set against the slim, elegant dark-lacquered chair and table. The well-used rocking horse at the foot of the bed is a conversation piece.

softer shade of pink, as harsh red is not flattering and can appear unfriendly.

Yellow on its own can give a sickly light, so for walls choose a soft, light yellow – not an egg-yolk shade – or a wallpaper with a white or off-white ground and a yellow motif. It is worth testing any potential yellows, both in daylight, particularly if the sun streams onto the walls, and at night, when the curtains are drawn and the light source is artificial. There are, of course, many pretty floral chintzes with green and yellows that are ideal for country bedrooms and, with restraint, town ones as well.

Green, rather like some blues, can also give the appearance of being cold and needs to be selected with care. It is a good colour in hot countries or in a beach house, but in a dreary northern climate can be a little sombre unless it is used in combination with other, warmer colours. Very pale pastel shades of green, such as a light eau-de-nil, work well with white or off-white, and evoke the Empire and Regency periods.

Until the advent of gas lighting in the Victorian era, most bedroom lighting was produced by candles, rush lights or tallow (fat) lamps; as late as the Empire period, oil lamps tended to be used in larger, public rooms. And it was only at the beginning of the twentieth century that reliable electric lighting was installed in most homes. The soft, subtle effect of the earlier indirect lighting suits bedrooms today, with wall brackets or sconces, standard and table lamps used in conjunction with – or even replacing – one or more pendant fixtures. Again, a number of lighting stores and mail-order companies specialize in period reproduction lights and lamps.

Opposite: This elegant bay window, with spectacular views over the countryside, is a perfect spot to place a piece of furniture on which to sit and enjoy the vista. This antique metal chaise is ideal because it is high enough, whereas regular armchairs would have been too low. The mattress is original buttoned horsehair, which gives a good, defined shape, and the pillows are also old. In this instance short curtains are appropriate as they leave the large radiator exposed.

Above: Where the surroundings are deliberately simple and plain, don't clutter up the feel with unnecessary patterning, even on small objects. A pure white jug is the perfect holder for the burst of colour provided by the flowers.

ATTIC ROOMS

Attic rooms are full of character, with irregular wall and ceiling lines and intermittent beams. They can be difficult to furnish, especially if the walls are steeply pitched, leaving you a small area in the centre with the only available headroom. Use dead space around the perimeter for low-level storage cupboards or low pieces of furniture.

When treating attic room walls, paint the walls and ceiling as one, rather than trying to define where one starts and the other finishes. With wallpaper, use a non-directional pattern that can also be used on the ceiling. Leave beams their natural colour, and it is worth sanding and stripping painted or blackened beams back to the original wood.

Attic windows can also be testing, especially if they are on a slope; roller blinds on runners, or ones that can be hooked down at night, are best. Dormer windows can have roller blinds or curtains on dormer rods that fold back into the recess.

Left: This bedroom, on the first floor of an old house, has an attic's intimacy, with a pitched ceiling and exposed beams. The oak door, floor and beams are all original, and their rich, antique patina, along with lime washed walls, create a sixteenth-century feel. The furnishings have been kept simple, with plain linen curtains on a metal pole and an antique crewel bedspread.

Right: In this simple, pale-furnished room, strong colours are confined to small cushions on the comfortable armchairs.

THE DETAILS OF DESIGN

Of all the features in a house, it is the details, of architecture and structure,

that hold the key to its first impression and reveal its true period. The details

of design create the tone of the house, and, while the architectural

details set the scene for the main interior, it is careful study of the past

that leads to the blend of authenticity with contemporary creativity

which makes for a successful period interior – whatever the style chosen

or imposed by the building itself.

Left: This Medieval-style door, surrounded by Gothic calligraphy, offers a period feel that still maintains a clean, modern look.

STAIRS

Opposite, left and far left: Staircases did not become an architectural feature until well into the seventeenth century; before then they were little more than functional oak blocks of wood set against the wall with open risers, more like a fixed ladder. Solid blocks of wood were then used, rather than separate treads and risers, as is now the standard. Earlier staircases were enclosed and in straight runs, with the spaces between the newel posts and the handrail that ran between the posts often filled in with plaster. In grander houses, stout carved balusters were more common, as were carved panels reflecting the wall panelling. The newel posts were often elaborately carved and depicted heraldic designs taken from the family's crest. Oak was the most popular wood used for both treads and risers and the balusters, or pine in more modest houses – this could be either painted or left exposed.

Above right: Before the eighteenth century many staircases were hidden, but they now became an important architectural feature of the house, leading off the main entrance hall. The designs became more elaborate and the balusters finer, with usually two or three per tread, and they were finished with a carved tread end. Handrails also became finer to match the balusters, and were always polished wood, while the balusters could be painted or polished.

Below right: Main staircases are generally situated in the centre of the house, with many rooms leading off them, and therefore need to be treated neutrally. If a staircase is part of the entrance hall, then it is sensible to have continuity and use the same decoration for both, or at least similar colour schemes. If the staircase is elaborate and an important architectural feature, I would tend to keep the walls simply painted so as not to detract from it: here, the panelling below the dado rail provides depth and colour.

CEILINGS

Once upper floors were created in houses, the underside became the ceiling of the room

below. The space between the beams was generally plastered and insulated with rushes

or straw; they were often carved, with chamfered edges, and the underside was carved

with elaborate motifs, repeated on carved bosses where beams and straps met.

Simple plaster ceilings with grid patterns and plaster bosses were introduced during

the Renaissance period. Ceilings were almost always whitewashed, with beams left

polished, or painted with trailing flowers and leaves. Later, decorative ceilings became

more refined, having flat plastered surfaces with applied mouldings. Early Georgian and

Palladian houses favoured geometric symmetrical designs using Classical motifs, often

Left: In early houses where the rooms were one storey only, ceilings did not exist. Effectively, the roof was exposed, and the underside was the ceiling with exposed beams, thatch or roof tiles. This tall drawing room uses the concept of a Medieval great hall, combining it with deep wooden ceiling pendants; these became common in grand houses in the early sixteenth century, and spread rapidly to manor houses and larger town houses.

Above right: Throughout the Medieval and Renaissance periods, there were varying fashions between painting beams and ceiling pendants, or leaving them their natural colour. In Tudor times the beams and pendants were often carved, with chamfered edges and the underside carved with elaborate motifs, which might be repeated on carved bosses where the beams and straps met.

kept white. During the Rococo period, the French influence for asymmetrical scrolls

and curves became popular, with details being picked out in gilt. By the late eighteenth

century, cornices were shallow and simple. Applied decorative details were picked out

in paint colours, and panels were decorated with scenes painted onto canvas and then

fixed with decorated mouldings.

Victorian ceilings were more robust and ornamental, with pre-cast mouldings, in

both plaster and papier-mâché, used. Anaglypta paper was applied to the flat part of the

ceiling, or in between panels for added texture.

The quiet atmosphere of the ceiling in the room beyond this arch, with simple, symmetrical plaster mouldings and plain surfaces between them, is a sharp contrast with the deep plaster flower heads on the underside, and the grotesque grinning lion's head surmounted by leaves on the arch itself.

Right: Cornices did not come into fashion until the mid-seventeenth century, often decorated with a frieze. Baroque ceilings became a riot of ornamentation, with the simpler strapwork of earlier eras giving way to flowing, natural lines.

LANDINGS AND LOFTS

The earliest English Building Acts in the eighteenth century were mainly concerned with

the size and interior arrangements of town houses; because space was at a premium,

these houses left little room for 'dead' spaces other than a basic hall and landing. So

whereas larger town and country houses might well have spaces that could be used as

vistas in themselves, in the towns these were largely confined to landings or lofts.

Whatever the space, even the usually cluttered Victorians recognized the need for

some areas that served no immediately useful purpose, and they can today act as

balances against overcrowding. They can blend in harmoniously with colour schemes, or

can be contrasted for maximum effect.

Left: The atmosphere in this landing is all about the contrast between the elegant, delicate balusters and curved handrail, and the dark oak of the Renaissance-style chairs. Both the light and dark colours are present in the rug.

Right: The symmetry of the balusters along the landing and the arched window with its attendant sidelights are the dominant features here. Drapes or curtains would obscure the clean, Palladian shapes, which include the raised-and-fielded panels on the door.

Top floors, lofts and attics are often open spaces waiting to be used, particularly today, when every room in a terraced house may be needed. Rather than attempting to obscure the room's origins, it is worth exploring which original parts, such as beams, rafters and joists, can be used as architectural features. The beam across the width of this room also serves as a demarcation line between the natural light and the parts that it cannot reach.

WALLS

The decoration and treatment of walls has changed and developed in tandem with the

evolution of houses throughout the different periods, and walls' flat surfaces have often

been the first place where new materials and ideas have been tried out.

Before and during the Medieval period, walls were little more than bare stone or flat

plaster, which was whitewashed or painted in a natural pigment finish. In some grander

houses walls may have been embellished with wall hangings or tapestries, but by and

large they were left bare.

Wood panelling was introduced in the Renaissance (Tudor and Jacobean) period to

help insulate the walls and as decorative cladding, and it was also used to form internal

partition walls. Early panelling was either full-height or up to the dado rail, with plaster

Below: The Renaissance panelling shows the warmth, comfort and coziness that centuries-old wood can create. Match this deep, dark, glossy surface with pale cream, textured distemper (seen in the tiny sitting room through the doorway) to offer an elegant, but rustic contrast.

Right: When a fireplace is of such a grand scale, allow it to dominate the room. However, despite its majesty, the cool stone and symmetrical design provide a surprisingly easy and elegant backdrop to the rest of the room; note how it pulls the pieces and colours together.

above; it was initially a series of simple boards set in between uprights and cross-members, and later developed into square panels with carved motifs, wainscoting, or linenfold design, the latter taking its inspiration from fabric wallhangings.

During this period, oak was the most commonly used wood for wall decoration and was invariably left unpainted, but during the Baroque period and afterward soft wood became more fashionable – partly because of its lower cost – and would frequently be painted with geometric designs and stencils. Tapestries and woven fabrics were often hung on walls in grander houses, and sometimes an alternative surface of embossed and tooled leather would be used above the panelling.

Early Georgian walls were panelled to the full height of the room, with the panels commonly divided into three sections, frieze, field and dado; softwoods such as pine or deal were most commonly used, and were painted in one colour. As the Empire period progressed, panelling was built only to dado height, with paint, fabric, or the recent invention of wallpaper used above the rail. Applied details, such as pilasters and other plaster mouldings, became popular, and the woodwork was picked out in different shades of paint colours.

This fashion continued throughout the eighteenth century, with the wood panelling replaced by applied plaster mouldings. Although stucco work had been used since the sixteenth century, when it was known as parget work, fine, decorative, hand-modelled plasterwork came into its own and became widely used during the Palladian period.

Right: This eighteenth-century New England bedroom exemplifies the fresh elegance that pale walls create for a restful environment. In a typical style that has been revived in modern times, the wall is painted one colour, cream shot through with a green tint, while wooden window frames and skirtings are matched to the blue in the Empire-style toile de Jouy that billows around the four-poster. Here, the plainness of the walls acts as a crucial contrast to the exuberant pattern and flowing drapery of the bed and focal canopy.

While often masculine in feel, panelling is appropriate for studies and libraries, but its use in this family sitting room is also ideal. Panelling creates an instant atmosphere of warmth and intimacy without a sacrifice of elegance or loss of structure in a room. It is best lit from side tables, as here, or from specially positioned spotlights and picture lights, all of which allow a gentle light back from the wall surface to shine across the room. In contrast to the angularity of the wood, the chairs used here are purposely rounded, well-upholstered and covered in pale, easy feminine fabrics; their gentle curves, textured throws and plump cushions also work as a contrast to the sharp lines of the fireplace. Any remaining hint of exclusive masculinity is counterbalanced by the witty addition of a thoroughly modern faux-leopard footstool.

This use of plasterwork was followed in the Neo-Classical period by pre-made

gypsum mouldings, a material particularly used and applied by the Adam brothers. To

emphasize the fineness of the mouldings, they would often paint the background in pale

pastel shades and leave the mouldings white to stand out.

The decoration of the walls was influenced by the trends of the period, and in the

Empire era imported wallpapers were utilized, with oriental designs and paint

techniques such as marblizing, tortoiseshell, woodgraining and *trompe l'oeil*. Print rooms,

studies and libraries were another fashionable way of displaying engravings that had

replaced tapestries as a popular way of covering walls, and many walls were adorned

with specially commissioned family portraits, landscapes or still lifes. In Victorian times

it was typical for walls to be divided into three sections: floor to dado, dado to picture

rail, and picture to cornice, even in medium-sized terraced houses. For most of the era,

the Victorians liked to use a combination of colours, textures and finishes on one wall,

incorporating painted or polished panelling, wallpaper and paint techniques. Flocked

and Anaglypta wallpapers were also popular. The development of mass-produced

steel engravings and, slightly later, photography, meant that many walls were

literally covered with images, both framed and unframed, often grouped by the

subject matter.

Left: With the advent of mass-manufacturing techniques and artificial dyes, wallpaper came to prominence in the nineteenth century. Original designs are still popular today, particularly delicate, rustic floral designs. Here, the sprigged flowers in delicate forget-me-not blue are ideal for an old bedroom; a small repeat pattern covers irregular walls well, and mid-blue is always restful.

Right: Hung behind a small table for protection, a panel of antique painted linen dresses the bedside. Painted linen was originally used as wall covering, and is the predecessor to modern wallpaper. Often sized and designed for each house, linen panels found popularity on the heels of the tradition of hanging walls with tapestries and carpets. Abstract designs of patterns and flowers were popular, and the fashion for Eastern styles of silk hanging, with intricate embroidered lilies, chrysanthemums and bamboo reeds, was revived in the latter nineteenth century. Here, the vintage linen has been allowed to show its age, its raw texture, and its sun-bleached blue and beige standing out against the freshness of the walls.

When decorating period rooms today, it is important to try and retain as many of the original details as possible, such as wall panelling. If this has been destroyed or removed, or is beyond repair, consider replacing it with new material in the authentic style. This can apply both to wood panelling or applied plaster mouldings. Generally speaking, plaster is less expensive than wood, if it is not too intricate a design, and can be a reasonable and authentic way of adding architectural detail to a plain room. Once it is installed, a variety of paint finishes can be applied.

With wood panelling, the most important decision is whether to paint or polish the panels; it is a false economy to select expensive oak and then cover it with paint, when a softwood such as pine is more appropriate for the finish you desire. Make sure that the wood you use has been well dried and seasoned in order to avoid excessive cracking as the moisture evaporates; architectural salvage and wood-recycling firms are good sources of seasoned wood.

Depending on the size and grandeur of your room, you may wish to create additional architectural features by adding pilasters or columns or by creating a niche or alcove. Again, many such decorative features are available as reproductions, and it is possible to find reprints of architectural pattern books from the eighteenth century onwards. In addition, don't always think of walls as having to be made up of a series of straight lines; curves or angles can make rooms more interesting and create specific areas for sitting or placement of furniture.

Left: This splendid example of Victorian panelling in a country-house library shows key nineteenth-century design features, such as the intricately carved vegetation around the mirror and bookshelf, the finials studding each corner, and the double-inset nature of each of the panels.

TEXTILES AND FABRICS

Early textiles were used mostly for practical purposes, and there was a limited choice, as

they were all handmade, and the area where you lived and the raw materials available also

influenced what could be obtained. If decorating a Renaissance, Tudor or Jacobean

house today, textiles and furnishings should be mainly of wool, heavyweight damasks,

and brocades and crewelwork. Some wall hangings or bed hangings may have been

handpainted rather than embroidered, especially in more modest homes. Although

houses of that era did not have many curtains, I tend to use simple wrought-iron or steel

poles rather than fussy pelmets. The bed would have sumptuous hangings. Walls may

Opposite left: A contemporary-style patterned-weave fabric with a striped background covers this upholstered wing chair. The cushion fabric is a typical damask, here a combination of cotton and viscose for added strength and wear. A matching flanged cord is used as piping.

Opposite right: A contemporary-style damask on a moiré background covers this sofa. Flanged cord helps to define the lines of the scroll arm, and a matching bullion fringe adds elegance to the base.

Right: A detail showing part of the swag and tail of a window treatment. The curtain fabric is a woven silk, and a plain contrasting green silk has been used to line the tails. The bullion fringe is used to trim them both and gives a better definition to the base. The scroll braid also defines the leading edges of the curtains.

Below: This country drawing room features all the items in the detailed shots, and shows how the room and the colours work as a whole. The basis of the colour scheme was the reproduction French-style Aubusson rug, which has a lovely subtle combination of greens, yellows and corals. The style of the room is typical of the late eighteenth century.

have been adorned with tapestries or painted wall hangings, and other than those, little

fabric was used, so for upholstered furniture again keep your choice simple, with the

emphasis placed on textures rather than patterns. Early colours were also much more

limited and subtle, with the use of natural dyes, so dark, richer, earthy tones are

preferential to lighter, modern pastels.

Seventeenth-century Baroque houses saw a large increase in the use of soft

furnishings, largely influenced by France and Italy, where expensive, luxurious fabrics

were being woven for the aristocracy and their grand homes. These were used on walls

Below: Set dramatically by the vivid yellow walls and festoons of canary silk, the tone of elegance and luxury, characteristic of the eighteenth century, continues in the contrasting yet luxurious fabrics of the sofas and chairs. Shades of white and yellow mix to create a lively, but cool and cozy, restful room.

Right: Inspired by the sculptures of the Classical world and the Renaissance, drapery as decor reached its peak in the salons of eighteenth-century America and Europe. Here, the lavish window treatment, with large windows swagged in yellow and braided in rich cream, maintains an easy elegance.

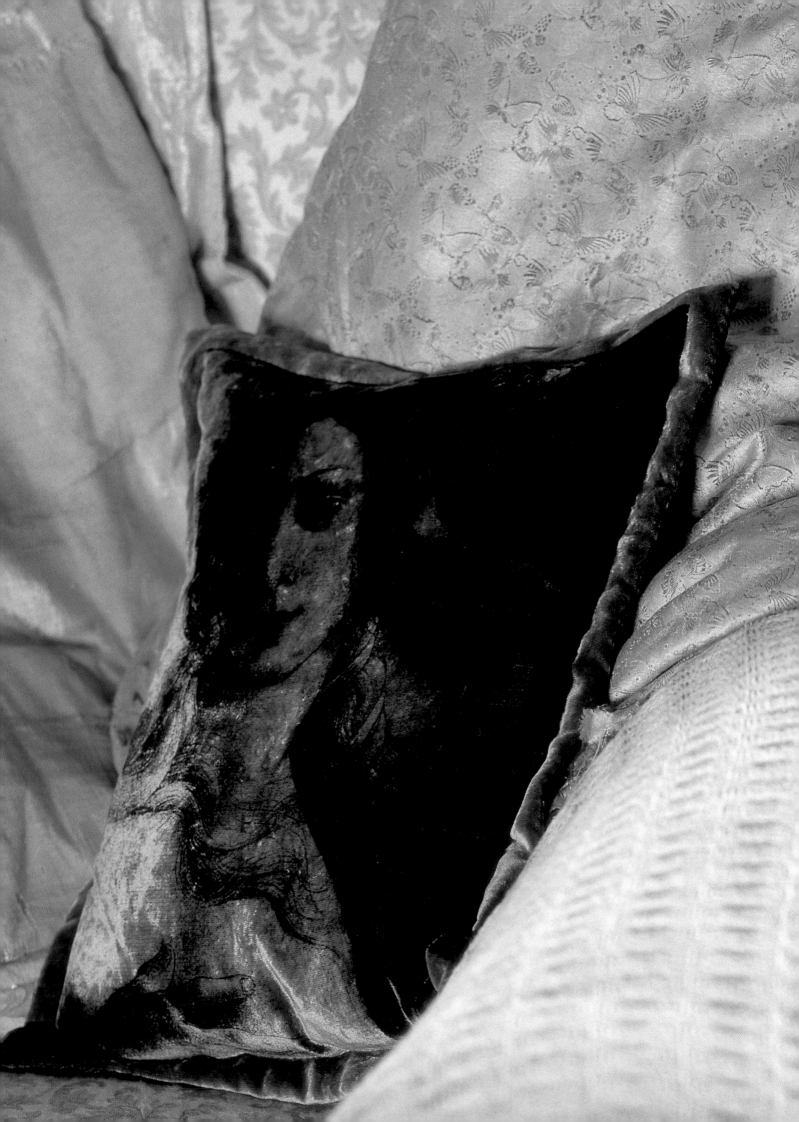

and for upholstery and bed curtains; window drapes were still uncommon. More

modest homes used predominantly woollen, linen or flax fabrics. Baroque rooms can be

large and imposing, so it is important to create a welcoming feel; for this, the use of

strong, bold colours and textures is better than lightweight pale silks. Walls should be

covered with wool damasks or adorned with tapestries or wall hangings. Keep the

treatment of the curtains simple – if you choose to have a pelmet or valance, then a

stiff, shaped one is more suitable than swags and tails.

The eighteenth-century Early Georgian era witnessed a greater emphasis placed on

comfort; and with entertaining at home coming more into fashion, houses had to be

practical and inviting. Living rooms were furnished with upholstered sofas and chairs,

typically covered in damasks, velvets and embroidered fabrics, with a secondary set of

lightweight slip covers in a check or stripe for summer use. Window treatments were

still relatively sparse at the beginning of the century, with festoon curtains or single

curtains hanging from rods. The curtain fabric was often the same as the walls, and

Above right: This room features the original plank wall and wooden oak floors from the sixteenth century. For this period, simple printed fabrics or plain weaves work best, with accessories of embroidered or tapestry cushions and throws. The antique rug helps to add warmth and a different texture into the room.

Left: A detail of the armchair shown on the opposite page, which is covered in a printed cotton fabric, similar to the early hand-blocked designs found in the seventeenth century. The simplicity of the designs allows for the use of other patterned cushions or, as here, a textured throw.

upholstery was typically of damask, until the increased production and importation of printed fabrics made them more readily and inexpensively available.

By the Regency and Empire periods, interior furnishings had reached a new height of elegance, with fabrics being used in abundance. Printed chintzes, cottons and silks were being imported from the East, while brocades and toile de Jouy came from France, and velvets from Italy. Although shutters were still commonly used for protection, most windows were dressed with curtains, and towards the end of the era it was not uncommon to have several layers of drapes: a pair of curtains with elaborate swagged pelmets trimmed with exotic tassels and fringes; a secondary layer of sheer or lightweight silk curtains; and possibly a roller or festoon blind.

Authentic fabrics, such as silk damasks and brocades, can be prohibitively expensive; as an alternative, I often recommend using a plain silk or man-made lookalike silk or taffeta for the curtains; if well-made and trimmed with elegant fringes and tassels, this can look the part. The same principle applies for upholstery: good-quality plain linens,

Above left: A silk damask fabric has been used for these rich curtains and swagged pelmet, which is attached to the curtain, as opposed to being separate, and hangs from a pole. The heavyweight bullion fringe and rope tassels add to the Victorian look.

Left: This window treatment has two sets of curtains, one short-draw and one long-dress. The fabric is wool paisley, which is trimmed in a three-colour fan edge and matching double-tassel tiebacks.

Right: This dining room is typical of the Victorian 'Jacobean' style, with a traditional oak refectory table and Victorian-style furnishings. The advantage of having the pelmet attached to the curtains is that with low ceilings and little space above the top of the window, little light is lost when the curtains are drawn back.

Below left and below right: Crewelwork or embroidered fabrics and throws were typical of the Tudor and Jacobean periods, and then again during the Arts and Crafts era. The embroidered antique quilt works well with the timber beams and simplicity of the other furnishings. Plain linen fabric has been used for the curtains, and rather than having a four-poster bed, a single curtain has been attached to the wooden beam, both as a decorative feature and to provide protection from the draughts.

Opposite: A contemporary crewelwork/embroidered fabric has been used to dress this picture window in a Welsh cottage. The Roman blind does not cut out much light or view, and the long-dress curtains, hung on a traditional wrought-iron pole, add warmth. The style is suitable for both period sixteenth-century rooms or later revived styles. The antique white lace bedlinen and antique Welsh quilt complete the look.

velvets and wools can be used for sofas and chairs, and more expensive brocades, brocatelles and embroidered fabrics for accent cushions or a throw-over tablecloth.

Victorian interiors and furnishings were much more flamboyant and eclectic. Textures and patterns played a large part, and rooms were crammed with overstuffed, deep-buttoned upholstered pieces covered with goffered velvets, damasks, paisleys, printed cottons and other fabrics, and trimmed with ropes, tassels and bullion fringes. Curtains were often multi-layered, with lace or voile curtains used for privacy in town houses, and heavy curtains with stiff, shaped pelmets and applied braids that often hung from a carved wooden pelmet, with ropes as decoration.

FURNITURE

It is virtually impossible to imagine a room without the comfort of upholstered furniture to sit on and wooden pieces for aesthetic and practical purposes, but this was the case in the Medieval period. Furniture evolved along with houses, as the desire for greater comfort developed and as influences and styles from different countries expanded craftsmen's skills and knowledge.

As a guideline, earlier houses from the fifteenth and sixteenth centuries, and of the Renaissance, Tudor and Jacobean styles, can be sympathetically furnished with oak pieces or the occasional piece of walnut. These houses work best with exposed oak beams, timber floorboards and panelled walls, and the scale should be kept appropriate. Mahogany was not used in great abundance until the Early Georgian era, and pieces such as long, extending dining tables did not exist until the mid-eighteenth century, and therefore would look incorrect in an earlier house.

By contrast, it is easier to use a long oak refectory table in a later house, especially a country cottage or farmhouse, where oak is more suitable. The disadvantage is that it is difficult to find comfortable antique oak dining chairs, as narrow benches, backstools or hard upright chairs were typically used. You may therefore have to opt for well-made reproduction ladderbacks or Windsor chairs with a loose cushion or squab seat.

Left: A typical Early Georgian living room on the *piano nobile* of an eighteenth-century house. The walnut tallboy, with brass drop-leaf handles and bun feet, is of the Queen Anne period, and is the ideal piece for this period room.

During the Empire era, furniture production was prolific and of supreme quality.

Early pieces were of walnut and fine and simple in design, reflecting the clean lines and

elegance of Queen Anne and Palladian houses. Cabriole legs were a characteristic feature

that was found on wing chairs, sofas and many types of tables.

During the Rococo period, the French style for opulence in design became popular

and very influential. Painted finishes combined with gilt were also popular. Most Early

and Mid-Georgian English pieces were made from mahogany, which allowed for the

production of large pieces such as bookcases and extending tables. Important

Below: Increasingly rare today, English Baroque furniture is renowned for its intricate grandiosity leavened with wit and playfulness. This fine side table, to be displayed in a plain hall, features the mythological sphinx at each corner; its considerable weight is borne by four small mahogany turtles. Revealing its enduring value, it is no less a novelty today than in the early eighteenth century.

cabinetmakers such as Thomas Chippendale became influential in furniture designs, but

the architect of the house was largely responsible for the design of many important

pieces. As the period progressed furniture became finer and was decorated with

marquetry and inlay, and satinwood was used for many smaller pieces. Robert Adam's

designs were typical of this Neo-Classical style, and his furniture included painted and

gilded pieces, such as consoles with mirrors above.

By the end of the Georgian period rosewood had become the favoured wood to make

Regency and Empire pieces, combined with more exotic woods, such as zebra, tulip and

Below: Colonial-style furniture is renowned for its clean lines, simplicity and focus on natural materials. Here, the placement of an early daybed draws attention to the main qualities of this period, echoing ideas in Georgian England: quality, delicacy and understatement blended to provide an impression of refined elegance and comfort.

maple, for inlay. Each piece of furniture was designed for a purpose, such as work

tables, games tables, chiffoniers for storage, sideboards and so on, and the pieces were

often decorated with brass grilles or a gallery. Designs were influenced by Greek,

Roman and Egyptian motifs, and furniture was now made to be freestanding, rather

than placed against a wall.

   Victorian furniture had to be designed and made to suit the larger, robust scale of the

rooms, so mahogany was the most used and suitable wood early on in the period.

Heavy turned and bulbous legs were common features on chair and table legs, and

dining chairs were typically balloon-backed. The fashion for Gothic and Elizabethan

Below left:: For many people, the key to making a success of period style involves working with pieces acquired over the years from family and partners, or purchased on an impulse. Here, a pair of Medieval-style hall chairs are sited alone for maximum impact.

Below right: This Georgian chair design was much copied in the nineteenth century, and also works in a set.

styles re-emerged, which led to many old pieces being remodelled with appropriate

carved motifs; alternatively, new, heavily carved oak pieces were manufactured, which

were dramatic to look at but uncomfortable to sit on.

Smaller pieces and decorative accessories became increasingly popular, such as papier-

mâché trays, chairs, boxes and so on, which were painted with flowers and inlaid with

mother-of-pearl. Other practical items included hat stands, Canterburies, hanging

shelves and firescreens. Brass beds were introduced, replacing the typical wooden

four-posters, and as everyday hygiene became more of a priority, bedrooms were

furnished with pretty washstands.

Below left: The chaise longue has undergone a revival in popularity. Placed in a bedroom, this typically Victorian striped and button-upholstered example returns to its roots as a daybed.

Below right: Sumptuous velvet, silk and textured covers can give a favourite chair a new lease of life, as well as allowing for seasonal changes.

WINDOWS

Windows in Medieval houses were little more than slits or openings. They did not

become glazed until Tudor times, when stone or wood mullions were introduced as

uprights in order to support the lintel of the window. At this time, the panes were one

Left: From an internal architectural point of view, windows tend to get ignored, and by and large they are covered with curtains or some type of window treatment, which is preferential for both aesthetic and practical reasons.

Below: By the 1790s, shaped windows such as arched, oriel, Gothic, bay and bow were all popular. They were used both as external and internal architectural features.

Right: Wrought-iron casement stays were produced in a variety of designs.

Below right: Where a window is an architectural feature, it can often be best to leave it without curtains or blinds, so as not to detract from its effect.

piece of glass. At the start of the seventeenth century, upright mullions were added with transoms – horizontal bars – and the criss-cross panes were replaced by larger, rectangular ones. As glass production advanced, the design of windows changed and opening casement windows were introduced

During the seventeenth century sash windows started to replace casements. The typical arrangement of panes was six over six, and windows were furnished with internal shutters. Because the frames were largely made of softwood, it was necessary to paint them with a white lead paint, which soon became a typical feature of Georgian windows. Towards the end of the century, as buildings developed and evolved so did the style of the windows. Many grander houses had the main rooms on the first floor, the *piano nobile*, and these rooms now had full-length windows which opened onto a terrace or balcony.

Throughout the nineteenth century, plate glass was introduced, and glazing bars became finer and glass panes larger, so the six-pane sash was more commonly replaced with four large panes, but this trend changed during the Victorian period, when sash windows were typically found with two large panes.

Left: In the Victorian era, just as new buildings were being built in Neo-Tudor, Jacobean and Gothic styles, there was accordingly a return to using casement windows and leaded lights, and metal frames replaced traditional wooden ones

Right and above right: How you paint window frames and sills is largely down to personal taste. The use of white paint has been popular since Georgian times, but there is no reason why windows should not be painted to match other coloured woodwork in the room, or left unpainted, to show the grain and colour of the wood, especially if it is a rich-coloured hardwood.

EXTERIOR DETAILS

Of all the features in a house, it is the exterior details that address the true style and period of the house and, crucially, set the scene for the interior.

Doors, windows and roofs should always be interesting architectural features. Each needs to be considered in context within the whole façade as well as individual features. Many of us take external features for granted: we naturally spend more time inside, so we appreciate interior details and features more readily. However, we should appreciate the importance of our first impressions and acknowledge those features that unite parts of the house to form one.

Frequently promoted as status symbols in the past, front doors have always been major focal points and play a key part in making the first impression of your house. One technique for providing a unity of style in

Top left:: The detail of this doorway was copied from Montacute House, a Jacobean house in Somerset, England. Although not the main front door, it remains an important feature, and accordingly its arched frame has been carved with strong details.

Left: This new French window is one of three that lead off the existing drawing room. The contemporary style is inspired by earlier Gothic designs to add interest both internally and externally.

the house is to use period ornaments on the front door. Cast-iron door knockers are suitable for periods up to the seventeenth century, while polished brass sets of letter box and door knocker create an eighteenth-century European feel even before guests have entered the house.

Windows add balance to the external façade and provide light and fresh air for the inside of the house. Accordingly, their location and size needs to be considered from both these points of view, which can sometimes cause conflict.

Roofs tend to be more of an architectural feature, rather than offering more than one practical function, although you should bear in mind that this can change if the attic area contains accommodation and the roof has dormer windows. However, you can emphasize roof features by using exterior paints in appropriate colours to pick out cornices, ledges and smaller carvings.

Top right: This roof detail is taken from a modern extension styled as a Medieval great hall. Both façade and roof are copied from the original Jacobean-style house, so the new and the old blend well.

Right: Because the hall and traditional beamed roof reach over two storeys, it is important that the doorway is in proportion. The door is of Jacobean oak, and the local stone was mined from the same quarry as that used in the original house built centuries ago.

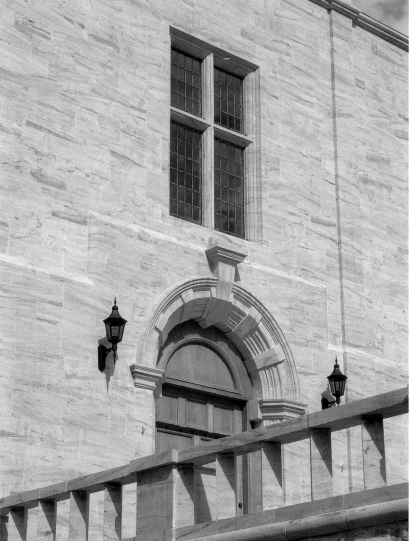

DOORS

Throughout the Georgian period, doors followed the classical rules of proportion, and

the panel sizes were adapted to suit the proportions of the room. The detail of the

mouldings used, such as egg and dart, was often taken from wall panelling in the room,

and the detail of the frames or architraves, and in grander houses over door pediments,

was sometimes taken from the fire surrounds. The architect or joiner took it upon

themselves to ensure that all the architectural details within a room were coherent.

In the early eighteenth century, fanlights became an important architectural element

of the front door, introduced to let daylight into the hall. Originally they were

rectangular, fairly simple in style and made of wood, but as the period progressed they

Below left: The shallow arched top to a door, typical of Medieval and Renaissance times, is known as a four-centred arch. The door surrounds, whether in timber or stone, often had carved spandrels, which in turn were dressed with a hoodmould. Hoods supported by carved brackets were popular during the sixteenth century, both as a decorative feature and as protection from the elements.

Below right: Early external doors were almost always solid-oak planks with horizontal battens laid across the back, held in place by wooden pegs or iron nails. The hinges and door furniture were in iron. Most Tudor and Jacobean doors had flat tops. Early front doors did not have knobs and knockers, as they were secured from the inside.

became more elaborate, often arched or semicircular, and with intricate metal detail.

Following on from the fanlight, glazed side panels were introduced to the front door, with the design often reflecting that of the fanlight.

Victorian front doors were built to be imposing and a status symbol, and many Victorian houses had raised ground floors so the entrance was approached up a short flight of stairs with an arched or Gothic-style porch. The front door was either painted a dark colour or wood-grained, and the glazed side panels and fanlight were frequently coloured or stained glass. Into the Arts and Crafts period, front doors became half-glazed, with the glazed top section depicting Art Nouveau patterns.

Below left: Glazed panels for doors and matching sidelight windows became popular in the late eighteenth century. Empire and Federal examples would often combine coloured glass. Their introduction allowed entrance halls and lobbies to be brighter without the use of a fanlight, which would be out of place in a low-ceilinged space.

Below right: In the sixteenth century, plank doors became replaced by panelled ones, which were single or double, depending on the grandeur of the façade. Linenfold and two-panelled doors were popular, and, in the seventeenth century, six-panel, raised-and-fielded doors became commonplace.

GARDEN ROOMS

Garden rooms and conservatories are wonderful additions to any house. While garden rooms are a natural extension of the house, generally built as a solid structure that blends with the existing architecture, a conservatory is an extension to a building.

The key to designing a garden room is to keep it simple. Treat this airy, sunlit space as a transition between indoors and the great outdoors, with an attendant consideration to informality and relaxation. Furniture should be made of natural materials, such as wood, cane, bamboo or wicker, or alternatively of rustic-style cast iron. Elaborate window treatments should be kept to the minimum: fussy festoon blinds or curtains do not work. For practical purposes, use little more than wood or pinoleum blinds fixed to the windows, and beneath the glass roof, if there is one, to protect the furniture and furnishings from sunlight. Plain blinds are preferable to patterns and coloured fabrics.

Left: This garden room was designed to blend in with the existing house. The same stone was used, rather than all glass, and sash windows and French doors match the house's period features. Only a glass conservatory roof has been used. Roof blinds are used as protection from the sunlight, while traditional chandeliers and wall lights provide the main lighting, boosted by accent lamps. The furniture is a combination of bamboo and cast iron, with a limestone floor.

Right: This typical Victorian-style garden room is very much part of the main house and is positioned to offer lovely views of the garden and valley beyond. Because it does not have a glass roof, it can be treated more as a sitting room, and is carpeted in wool, with upholstered furniture and fabric curtains.

The best garden rooms and conservatories are floored in hard materials, such as tiles, stone or brick. Wood is not a practical choice, as it moves and warps during damp weather and seasonal fluctuations in temperature. To heat your room, I recommend either an underfloor system or pipework heating around the room's perimeter, disguised with cast iron grilles. Radiators can be unsightly, and there may well be no spare wall space upon which to hang them.

With their glass roofs and small wall surfaces, lighting garden rooms can be tricky. Wall lights are always a good choice, as well as a focal centre light attached to the roof structure. Alternatively, you might try to conceal lights behind plants and furniture. When you are in the planning stages, bear in mind that it is useful to install floor sockets for table lights. Remember that ornate lighting, in particular a chandelier, can be a fine addition; the light will glitter against the glass in a very romantic way.

Of course no garden room is complete without greenery. For practical purposes, do install a tap (faucet) for watering your host of greenery close by. When you choose plants for the room, you might try picking a selection of scented plants that offer their perfumes up at different times through the year; if you position them at the far end of the room, your guests will be encouraged to explore right to the end of your garden room, rather than stay in the main house. Conversely, try to group the rest of your greenery in full view of the rest of the house so it remains constantly appreciated.

Left: The natural stone walls and stone floor of this attractive garden room give a rustic feel. Appropriately, the furniture is in natural bamboo. The floral chintz adds warmth, while keeping the overall theme. It is not necessary to have any window treatments here, as the room is not overlooked, and because the roof is solid, bleaching by sunlight is not a problem.

GLOSSARY

ARCHITRAVE moulding around an arch, window or door

ARRAS a rich tapestry fabric hung on walls, usually depicting figures and scenes

ASHLAR FACING square-hewn stones, either applied to walls or laid in horizontal courses with vertical joints

BALUSTER a slender, upright post that helps to support a rail; or a short pillar or column with a circular section and curved profile

BALUSTRADE a series of balusters with a rail or coping attached to the tops

BAS-RELIEF a sculpture, carving or moulding with a low relief

BOSS an ornamental ceiling projection

CABRIOLE a curved leg of a piece of furniture, introduced during the Queen Anne and Early Georgian periods

CAME in a leaded window, a lead strip that holds plain or stained glass in a groove

CAPITAL a head or cornice of a pillar or column

CASING the whole wooden lining of a window or door

COFFER a sunk, ornamental wooden or plaster panel in a ceiling or soffit

COLUMN a vertical pillar, often tapering, used either separately as an ornament, or as part of a colonnade or arcade

CONSOLE an ornamental bracket supporting a bench; or a table supported by such brackets; or (modern) a cabinet containing electronic equipment

CORNICE an ornamental moulding that runs continuously along the meeting point of a wall and ceiling; or a picture rail

CORONA a part of a cornice that has a broad vertical face, usually projecting outwards

COVING a proprietary moulding used to make a cornice

DADO the lower part of an interior wall when coloured or covered differently from the upper part; often separated by a dado rail

DADO RAIL a moulding on a wall used to protect the wall from damage from furniture pushed against it

EAVES a projecting edge of a roof that overhangs a building

ENCAUSTIC on bricks and tiles, decorated with a variety of coloured clays by inlaying and burning into the surface

FILLET a narrow band that separates two mouldings; or a band between column flutes

FLANCH on the outside of a chimney shaft, the slope inwards towards the top; also flaunch

FLUTE a semicircular groove along the length of a column, or a vertical or horizontal length of wood in furniture

FRESCO a technique of wall painting where the paint is applied to freshly applied plaster before it dries

FRIEZE a wide horizontal band of decoration, usually painted or sculpted, near the ceiling at the top of an interior wall; also a strip of paper used thus; or sculpture filling the space between architrave and cornice at the top of a wall

HIGHBOY US term for a high chest used in bedrooms in the eighteenth century

INTARSIA inlaid mosaic decoration made of wood, stone, metal or glass

JAMB a vertical side piece on which the lintel sits in a doorway or window opening, or in a mantelpiece

LATH AND PLASTER a building technique for making a wall or partition by covering thin, narrow strips of wood with a layer of plaster

LINENFOLD a carved or moulded ornament that represents a scroll or fold of linen, usually on wood or plaster panels

LINTEL a horizontal supporting piece above a doorway or window opening

LOWBOY US term for a dressing table used in bedrooms in the eighteenth century

LUNETTE an arched opening that lets in light in a concave ceiling; or a semicircular or crescent-shaped space in a ceiling or dome, decorated with sculptures or paintings; also the pieces placed or painted in this

MARQUETRY a decorative technique for inlaying wood, ivory, etc. in a flat surface of wood; see also parquetry

MOULDING an ornamental variety of outline in capitals and cornices; also in wooden panels and furniture; or a strip of wood, metal, plaster, etc. applied and used as decoration

MULLION a vertical strip that divides the pieces of glass in a window frame

NEWEL POST a post that supports the handrail at the head or foot of a staircase; or the central supporting pillar of a spiral staircase

OVERMANTEL a piece of ornamental cabinetwork placed over a mantelpiece, often with a mirror

PARGETING an obsolete term for any plaster on a wall or ceiling, especially ornamental; or internal render on a chimney

PARQUETRY as for marquetry, except that the inlays are geometrical

PATERA (PL. PATERAE) an ornamental form that resembles a shallow dish; also a flat, round ornament in bas-relief

PILASTER a rectangular pillar or column that projects from a wall; or a cylindrical shape

RAFTER one of a series of sloping wooden beams that forms the framework of a roof and is covered by tiles, slates, thatch, etc., often exposed in Medieval houses

RELIEF a technique of moulding or carving where the design stands out from the plane surface in a solid form

REVEAL the vertical side of an opening in a doorway or window

SASH a wooden frame in a window, opened and closed vertically along grooves in the frame

SCAGLIOLA plasterwork produced to imitate stone and marble from the eighteenth century

SCONCE an ornamental bracket for holding one or more candles, fixed to an interior wall

SILL a horizontal strip of wood or stone that forms the bottom part of a window opening or doorway; or a threshold of a doorway or gateway

SOFFIT the underside of any architectural structure, such as an arch, balcony or cornice; also a board attached to rafters beneath the eaves of a roof

SOLAR the name for the main upper room in a Medieval manor house

SPANDREL the space between the outer curve of an arch and the rectangle formed by mouldings enclosing it, such as a wall and ceiling; or the generally triangular area between a set of steps and the ground

STILE a vertical piece in the frame of a sash window or panelled door

STRAPWORK decorative strips of folded or interlaced wood, metal or embroidery

STRING-COURSE a band of masonry or bricks that projects slightly from the surface of a wall

STUCCO a fine plaster made from pulverized marble and gypsum, used as wall and ceiling covering and for making decorative mouldings, cornices, etc.; also the decoration or ornamentation produced in this way

SWAG an ornamental moulded or carved representation of flowers, foliage or fruit; also curtains or drapery arranged to hang like this

TRANSOM a horizontal strip of wood or stone across a mullioned window, or between a window and fanlight

ACKNOWLEDGMENTS

The Author and Publishers would like to thank all those who kindly allowed their houses to be photographed for this book. The Publishers would like to thank Mr and Mrs John Tiffin, Miss Rose Hammick, Mrs Pippa Lewis, and Miss Karen Howes. Particular thanks are extended to Mrs Trish Storey, who created the Chinoiserie walls seen first on pages 26–29. She undertakes commissions and can be contacted at The First Impression, Old Berry Hill House, Westcott, Surrey, RH4 3JU, England, tel: 01306 882075, fax: 01306 882206. The Publishers would particularly like to thank Andrew Wood, who took many of the photographs for this book.

Photographic acknowledgments:

All photographs by Andrew Wood and are © Cico Books, except those that appear on the following pages:

18, 20, 21, 100–101, 158 – © Christopher Simon Sykes, The Interior
       Archive
30, 33, 87, 103, 138–39, 159 – © Ianthe Ruthven, The Interior Archive
38, 40, 41, 64, 70–71, 88–89, 140–41, 148–49, 172–73 – © Mick Hales
105 – © Andreas von Einsiedel
174–175 – © Lewis, Darnley, Edifice Picture Library